Restoring Balance to a Mother's Busy Life

Beth Wilson

CB
CONTEMPORARY BOOKS
A TRIBUNE COMPANY

Library of Congress Cataloging-in-Publication Data

Saavedra, Beth Wilson.
    Restoring balance to a mother's busy life /
Beth Wilson Saavedra.
        p.   cm.
    ISBN 0-8092-3196-4
    1. Motherhood.   2. Mothers—Psychology.
3. Mothers—Health and hygiene.   4. Self-help
techniques.   5. Rites and ceremonies.   I. Title.
HQ759.S15   1996
306.874'3—dc20   96-8169
                                      CIP

Material from *Grandmothers of the Light* by Paula Gunn
Allen reprinted by permission of Beacon Press.
    Material by Julia Cameron reprinted by the
permission of The Putnam Publishing Group/Jeremy P.
Tarcher, Inc. from *The Artist's Way* by Julia Cameron.
Copyright © 1992 by Julia Cameron.
    Material from *Raising Your Spirited Child* by Mary
Sheedy Kurcinka, copyright ©1992 by Mary Sheedy
Kurcinka, reprinted by permission of HarperCollins
Publishers Inc.
    Material from *Gift from the Sea* by Anne Morrow
Lindbergh, © 1978, reprinted by permission of Random
House, Inc.

Cover design by Kim Bartko
Cover illustration by Margaret Spengler
Interior design by Mary Lockwood

Published by Contemporary Books
An imprint of NTC/Contemporary Publishing Company
Two Prudential Plaza, Chicago, Illinois 60601-6790
Manufactured in the United States of America
International Standard Book Number: 0-8092-3196-4
10   9   8   7   6   5   4   3   2   1

To my son, Alexander, who challenges me
to ask the deeper questions and to be more
patient with living the answers. I love you.

To Jim, my beloved. Thank you for loving me
with the enthusiasm of a child, and the honest
commitment of one whose heart is true.

To the mothers of the world. Do not forget
the enormous contributions you make by being
a mother. According to Native-American
author Paula Gunn Allen, becoming a mother
is "the most important event in a woman's life."
In her book *Grandmothers of the Light*, she
describes the rigors of motherhood from a
medicine woman perspective: "In this period
she learns the discipline of sacrifice: her body,
her time, her nutrients, her psyche, her
knowledge, her skills, her social life, her
economic capacities, her relationships, and her
spiritual knowledge and values are all called
into the service of her children. This passage,
ambivalent at best, pushes her to reach beyond
whatever limits she thought she labored within,
making her stronger. . . ."
    Value your gifts and send them out into
the world with love.

Contents

Acknowledgments

To my mother, Anne, and my Grandma Mamo, who had me in hot springs and atop horses before I could walk, I thank you for teaching me ways to feed my soul.

To my father, Paul, and my Grampie Bud, I give abundant thanks for your constant, unwavering love, and I thank you for teaching me to value the rich solace and beauty of nature.

Thank you to my stepmother, Linda, and my Grammie Dot for their keen minds and common sense. You've helped me blend practicality with the yearnings of my heart.

To Patricia, Joey, and Colette LoConte who have welcomed Alexander and me into their lives, we are deeply grateful.

To know another's soul and have yours known is one of life's greatest gifts. Jillian Klarl and Todd Nelson have shared this gift with me. I love you both.

I am blessed with longtime friends who are to me as true sisters should be. Thank you for your inspiration, encouragement, enthusiasm, humor, and joie de vivre: Rose Benstock, Linda D'Agrosa, Nancy Edison, Betsy Allen, Ginger Hinchman, Morgan Soderberg, Jessica Donnelly, Caroline Douglas, Maris Allen, Lee Cook, Daryn Stier, and Marie Hartley.

Thanks to my "more recent" friends who travel the path of motherhood with me: Christine Ciavarella, Shirley Luna, Pia Hultqvist, Homa Tavana, and Diana Cope. I extend a special thank-you to Catherine Athans. She has helped me to traverse the threshold into adulthood, and her many talents have helped me to heal and become more whole.

My dear friends Eric Lieberman and Brad Pearsall have been wonderful additions to my life. I can't wait to see what you two are going to be when you grow up!

I am thankful for Alexander's teachers at Ananda school: Barbara and Colette Rabin. Their inspiration, perceptiveness, and kindness have helped Alexander to flourish and become the best that he can be.

I am fortunate enough to be close friends with some of my best friends' parents. They have taken me under their wing, and yet always treated me as an equal. To Hugh Donnelly, the only man who still affectionately calls me "Baby Doll," I extend a warm hug of thanks. To Nancy and Dick Allen who have opened their hearts and their homes to me, a heartfelt thanks. And, to the late Ilene Edison, a loving thanks. I will miss you. Your presence will endure in my life.

To my agent, Linda T. Mead, I thank you for your perseverance and continued enthusiasm.

Thank you to Nancy Crossman for your enthusiasm, intelligence, and hard work. I look forward to collaborating with you in the future. And, to the many people at Contemporary Books, particularly Alina Cowden and Dawn Barker, who continue to make me feel welcomed "to be on board," thank you.

Last, thanks to Nana Christiansen and Natasja Angenent for coming into our family and caring for Alexander in such a loving way.

Introduction

As soon as the newborn child—soft, wrinkled, and shockingly alive—is placed in a mother's arms, her world is permanently altered in ways she will continue to discover daily for the rest of her life.

Linda Burton, coauthor,
What's a Smart Woman Like You Doing at Home?

The first few days of my child's life, I was so exhausted I could not believe I'd survive until he was eighteen. It took no time at all to realize that my mothering skills were incomplete at best, and woefully inadequate when it came to dealing with the more challenging aspects of motherhood such as colic and erratic sleep patterns. "Why had I been permitted to return home from the hospital without taking one of the experienced members of the staff with me?" I wondered. "How was I going to care for this tiny being all by myself?" I had received no preparation for, or initiation into, this life-changing event, and, like it or not, as I quickly discovered, babies didn't come with operating instructions. Without warning, my world had been turned upside down. There were constant demands on my time. My sleep was being interrupted. Within the course of one hour I experienced a flurry of emotions ranging from bliss to anger to frustration. Add to that the fact that a twenty-inch person with a voracious appetite had me tethered to my couch, and the prospect of life as a mother became very unsettling.

Why hadn't anyone told me how dramatically my life would change? Why didn't anyone impress upon me the magnitude of what I was getting into? I had always heard mothers say that pregnancy was the easy part. But, until my son was born, I had no idea what they meant. Now it was my turn to experience initiation by fire. It was as if I was expected to know exactly what to do by virtue of my sex, and if I didn't know, I could become an "instant mother" simply by reading a few books and buying the proper baby equipment. Yet, as all mothers know, having a baby doesn't automatically transform one into an expert. As columnist Sydney J. Harris so aptly states: "The common fallacy among women is that simply having children makes one a mother—which is as absurd as believing that having a piano makes one a musician."

I began to question myself, wondering if I had been duped. Or, perhaps, I was just going about it all the wrong way. Something that worked one day didn't work the next. I couldn't always decipher a cry of hunger from tears caused by a wet diaper. Sometimes I would manage to complete household tasks despite my infant's need for constant holding; other times I had no idea where the day went. Obviously, *my* natural instincts weren't completely intact like all the other mothers whom I imagined were having an easier time of it. Otherwise, the events of my day would be flowing more smoothly. Or so I thought. Slowly, as I began to speak with mothers from a variety of backgrounds, it became apparent that my situation was not unique. All of us were experiencing the same challenges and joys—the frustration as well as the bliss. And we were all working hard to combine the various aspects of our lives into a workable format so that we could navigate through motherhood without losing our sanity.

Exploring other cultures and traditions I discovered that, until recently, women were assisted through this journey into motherhood and supported by the community or tribe well into their children's young lives. Unlike women today who are often feeling their way in the dark, mothers of the past received ample instruction and nurturing assistance. For example, among the Aborigines all brothers and sisters of the new mother are considered to be aunties and uncles with similar, if not identical, responsibilities as the birth parent. The role acquired by these relatives extends far beyond our current concept of uncle and aunt. The child is actually believed to have several mothers and fathers depending on the size of the woman's family. In addition, all children are considered to be the responsibility of the community. Thus, if a mother feels compelled to go on a walkabout (a solo spiritual quest out in the Australian bush where a person may stay away for days or even months at a time), her child is cared for by the tribe's "mothers" and "fathers," namely her sisters and brothers, as well as grandparents and other relatives. Since the child receives ample love and affection from others besides his birth mother, neither the mother's needs nor the child's needs are sacrificed.

In some African cultures a mother's physical needs are met by the tribal community, especially during the first few months of her baby's life. Knowing that this time can be the most overwhelming as the mother attempts to balance her child's needs with her other daily obligations, members of the tribe wash her clothes, prepare her meals, and assume her farming chores. Not only does this allow the new mother time to rest adequately and heal after the birth, it also gives her a chance to focus on her baby, learning from more experienced women how to care for her infant.

In the Jewish tradition, other women, be they sisters, aunts, grandmothers, or close friends, assist the mother as she makes the transition into motherhood. The constellation of women surrounding her give their time and expertise, providing support and advice for the new mother, as well as teaching her a variety of ways to handle situations that arise in the early years. Given this circle of confidants, she is less likely to feel isolated, overwhelmed, or helpless as she encounters the challenges of motherhood.

Unfortunately, today, these networks of seasoned women are not readily available. Systems of support formerly provided by the community no longer exist. As Clarissa Pinkola Estes, author of the bestselling book *Women Who Run with the Wolves*, points out: "In most parts of the industrialized countries today, the young mother broods, births, and attempts to benefit her offspring all by herself. It is a tragedy of enormous proportions." What is the result? Mothers tend to question themselves, wondering what they are doing wrong and why they can't keep up with the enormous demands, not realizing that over the years the community has fallen away, leaving more and more gaps to be filled by mothers. It is no wonder mothers are often overtaxed and overburdened, and yet they strive to keep up, responding to images of Superwoman instead of learning to take care of themselves in meaningful ways. As Jennifer Louden, author of *The Women's Comfort Book*, attests, women are conditioned to meet everyone else's needs before their own and believe that the people in their lives will likewise anticipate and meet their needs. "When this does not happen," according to Louden, "we begin to feel we have no right to our needs and desires. What we end up with is women who are experts at nurturing others—until we drop of exhaustion or illness or escape into excessive drinking, shopping, or eating."

Our entry into motherhood means we must learn how to make sacrifices for our children without sacrificing ourselves. This is no easy task considering the complexity of our lives.

Yet, we need to make time for ourselves—to create a safe place where our inner lives can be nourished, our bodies and minds replenished, and our spirits renewed. We need to rediscover the lost art of mothering; mothering ourselves so that we can, in turn, fully mother our children and absorb the rich experience of motherhood. For this reason, *Restoring Balance to a Mother's Busy Life* not only provides concrete methods for nurturing mothers, but helps to create a new paradigm for mothering that involves one's partner, one's family, and one's community. *Restoring Balance to a Mother's Busy Life* contains meditations to reflect on throughout the day; advice from other mothers; brief "chicken soup" rituals to soothe and lift a mother's spirits, pertinent information on topics such as postpartum depression, sex, and maintaining one's identity; writings that validate the many feelings and experiences only mothers are privy to; as well as creative suggestions designed to help a woman navigate through each day in a way that respects and enhances her unique, personal style of mothering. You will also find exercises on setting boundaries, prioritizing your needs as well as your family's, and trusting your instincts. Last, I have included practical assistance in the form of resource lists and step-by-step suggestions for tackling a plethora of issues: child care, division of household chores, and methods for enjoying yourself while you are with your children, to name a few.

I encourage you to use this book as a tool—a tool for restoring balance even when the whirlwind of activity threatens to pull you farther and farther from yourself; a tool for learning how to better care for yourself; a tool for remembering who you are inside, as a mother and an individual; and a tool for helping you appreciate and value your own worth.

Magic Circle Time

In the sheltered simplicity of the first days after a baby is born, one sees again the magical closed circle, the miraculous sense of two people existing only for each other.

Anne Morrow Lindbergh

The sacred time between a mother and her newborn infant is like no other time. A magical circle surrounds us as though we exist only for each other. Our eyes speak with the love of our hearts, and we begin to form a bond—our special, shared journey—that will last for the rest of our lives. We bask in what Anne Morrow Lindbergh calls, "the sheltered simplicity of the first days." Time is inconsequential, and the world shrinks into the microcosm of mother and child while expanding to take in the enormity of our new commitment and our devoted love for our little baby. We are suspended in the womb of each other's company, and together we introduce ourselves to each other in the gentlest of ways: holding, stroking, rocking, nursing, singing, and cooing.

This sacred time is also a time of healing and rest, giving our bodies time to be quiet and safe in our homes. It is a time to ask for help with meals, laundry, and phone calls and not feel guilty about it. This is when we quiet our minds and relax our tired, labor-worn muscles. For many it is also an important time for crying tears of joy, relief, and sorrow, and for feeling abundant bliss. Our lives have changed dramatically in a matter of hours, and we feel the profound reverberations of this passage on every level of our being. Now is the time to honor the magnitude of this passage and to celebrate the miracle of birth—the birth of our child and the birth of ourselves, as mothers—by being aware of the moment and experiencing its exquisite vitality.

Sacred Time Ritual:
Keep It Simple

Purpose:
To Attend to the Magic of the Present

Place your favorite guided meditation tape in a tape player or Walkman (suggestion: Before the birth of your child, tape your *own* voice reading your favorite guided meditation, poems, or quotes). Climb into your most comfortable rocking chair. Make sure your clothes are loose and soft against your skin. Take several deep breaths, making sure you exhale completely. You may wish to sigh or make a sound of release such as "aaahhh." Then rock, slowly, allowing your mind to swirl with magical thoughts and images, leaving no room for "I should be preparing dinner," "I should probably check on the baby," etc. Just rock to the same gentle rhythms you use when lulling your baby to sleep.

Bonding with Baby

In an age when we are told that good mothering is just a matter of finding the right sitter and learning to arrange "quality time," most of us could never have envisioned how completely we would be taken by these delicious miniature people.

Linda Burton, coauthor,
What's a Smart Woman Like You Doing at Home?

It is easy to become completely swept up in the excitement of becoming a mother. What most of us don't anticipate is the amount of stress we will encounter in the first few weeks after our child's birth. If we don't get in the habit of caring for ourselves early on, we will quickly exhaust our resources, and it will become exponentially more difficult to catch up because we have to care for an infant. Studies indicate that there are two important factors to consider in preventing postpartum depression: get enough assistance from others right from the start so our body has adequate time to recuperate, and keep our stress levels low as our hormonal system attempts to normalize.

The two following lists give examples of the different kinds of stress new mothers must contend with: positive stress and negative stress. Negative stress is usually easier to identify. However, prolonged positive stress can have negative results.

3

Like negative stress, positive stress overtaxes our system. If we do not make a conscious effort to minimize our stress levels, eventually we will be unable to adequately cope with the demands of motherhood.

In an age where the exchange of information is instantaneous, we often expect ourselves to absorb things at an incredible rate. But, we are not computers. We need time to assimilate the awe and wonder, the excitement and fear. We need to catch our breath. For these reasons, we would do well to monitor our stress levels and give ourselves the time to take in the monumental changes that our baby brings.

Use these two lists as starting points for reviewing the stress in your life. Feel free to add to them. If two or more of these stress factors apply to you in any given day, schedule some time to return your focus to yourself and your newborn by following the ritual included in this chapter.

Positive Stress

- Friends and family calling and coming over to congratulate you
- Trouble sleeping owing to excitement
- Avoiding naps because you want to look at your baby
- Wanting to tell everyone everything about the birth and your baby within the first week
- Arranging and rearranging your baby's room (putting new clothes away, finding the exact spot for that stuffed bear Aunt Sylvia gave to your little one, etc.)
- Feeling so amorous and overjoyed that you want to make love with your partner instead of sleeping
- Thinking you have so much more energy than everyone told you you would that you make too many plans, write out too many announcements, and try to get started on your weight loss program too soon, etc.

- Feeling so dramatically changed by motherhood that you are compelled to record every event, every feeling, every photographic moment, everything

Negative Stress

- Feeling guilty about saying "no" to visitors
- Not knowing how to say "no" to others' demands
- Feeling guilty that the animals in the house aren't getting enough attention (St. Francis of Assisi syndrome)
- Feeling guilty about being worn out and cranky when your partner returns home at the end of the day
- Feeling isolated in the house all by yourself
- Feeling disappointed and guilty that staying home with baby may be less fun and more work than originally fantasized
- Feeling you are a "bad mother" if you aren't totally enamored of your infant every minute of every day
- Expecting yourself to maintain your life-before-baby routine no matter how challenging child care is
- Feeling frustrated that pumping breast milk isn't going as smoothly as you thought it would and so starting to believe you will never leave the house or have time away from your baby ever again (or feeling easily discouraged by new things, making it difficult to envision anything changing in the near future)
- Expecting yourself to keep up with housework and cooking while caring for an infant

This is not the time to let your mind seize the opportunity to drive you crazy. This is not the time to fall into the perfect-mother syndrome (you have plenty of time for that—the rest of your life!). This is not the time to compare yourself to others or to past performances. In the past you may have run a small business, organized an art exhibit, or waited on fifteen tables at the same time, but motherhood is different. Your previous work skills do not automatically transfer over and, chances are, you will have to learn some new skills—each in their own time.

Take this time to slow down and nurture the special bond between you and your child. Move at a snail's pace and let that be enough.

> ## Bonding with Baby
>
> ### Purpose:
> ### *To Honor the Special Bond Between Mother and Child*
>
> Lie down on your bed. Place your child next to you. Turn on your side, facing your newborn baby. Gently touch your fingertips to your baby's. Then, with your fingertips, stroke your baby's face, arms, legs, back and neck, recording and absorbing each aspect of your child through your fingertips. Then touch your own body in the same tender way. Caress it with your fingertips and thank it, with words or thoughts, for bringing this new being into the world. Feel the softness of your skin, the fullness of your breasts, the roundness of your hips and belly. Feel how perfect both of you are. Remember this feeling.

Things You Can Do to Enhance Bonding Time

• Have a friend or relative prepare meals for you and your family. If you can't find any volunteers, consider ordering in one meal a day, or as often as your budget will allow, for the first few weeks.

- Place on your door a picture of your newborn along with a gently worded request for privacy—"Quiet please. Mommy and I are resting after our great adventure in the hospital. If you'd be so kind as to stop by later, we'd appreciate it."
- Record a message on your answering machine that gives a brief description of your baby and a time frame for returning phone calls. Example: "Lily Ann has landed. She's a beautiful seven-pound, twelve-ounce baby girl. We can't wait to speak with you in person. For now, please be patient as it could take us a week or two to return the large number of phone calls we've received. Thank you for calling."
- Wait to send out announcements. Believe it or not, there is no rush. Your closest friends and relatives will get all the news via the grapevine. It's not your job to fill everyone in *immediately*.

Resource:

Sears, Martha, and William Sears, M.D. *25 Things Every Mother Should Know*. Boston, MA: Harvard Common Press, 1995.

Organizing Help

Of all the passing notions, that of a human being for a child is perhaps the purest in the abstract, and the most complicated in reality.

Louise Erdrich

I cannot stress enough how essential it is to enlist the help of friends, relatives, mother's helpers, baby-sitters, doulas, mothers' groups, and whomever else you might need, *before* your baby arrives. And while all mothers need assistance, in particular, single mothers and those women whose partners are frequently out of town must have a network of support in place. Otherwise, it is too easy to become overwhelmed and isolated. An African proverb says, "It takes an entire village to raise a child." Not only will the assistance of others significantly diminish the chances of postpartum depression, but it will also enable you to more thoroughly enjoy your entrance into motherhood and to more confidently adapt to your new role as a mother.

Since many may not be familiar with the various options available, I have put together a list of possible helpers ranging from doulas to neighborhood teenagers, and have included some ideas for how you might make use of their services or assistance.

9

The doula. The *doula*'s primary function is to provide support for the entire family, and she can do this in a variety of ways: cooking, cleaning, shopping, doing the laundry, answering the phone, running errands, helping with older siblings, caring for the new baby, and fielding visitors. Perhaps more important, the doula is available to offer emotional and moral support, advice on breast-feeding or bottle-feeding, massage, and lessons on basic infant care. Some doulas offer special services such as cooking vegetarian meals, keeping a kosher home, or planning and preparing menus and meals. In her book *Mothering the New Mother*, Sally Placksin puts it like this: "She is there to facilitate your time to settle in, relax, and heal, while assuring that the daily underpinnings of your life remain anchored as much as possible. . . . She is the peace-of-mind factor." In short, the doula can be a mother, best friend, and confidant rolled into one.

What should you look for when choosing a doula? Non-judgmental support, the ability to be attentive and to anticipate needs, and a strong, comfortable, and friendly rapport are three important factors many mothers mentioned. Finding a doula whose belief system is closely aligned with your own is essential. That way, there will be little friction, possibly none at all, concerning the choices you make: to breast-feed or bottle-feed, to take extended periods of time alone, to adhere to certain diets, and so on. Considering the amount of unsolicited advice you'll probably receive, this will be a welcome relief!

The ability to be attentive and anticipate another's needs is quite an art form. It makes others feel truly cared for and nurtured. A mother who is receiving this type of support is less likely to feel as though she is "asking" for help or giving orders, and so she can be more relaxed. A doula who has these qualities makes it easier for a mother to "go off the clock" because she is assured that all is taken care of, and she need not always be the one in charge.

A good rapport is indispensable. After all, the doula will be an integral part of your family's life during an intensely emotional time. Do you feel at ease knowing this person will become a part of your family temporarily? (For some mothers, a lasting bond with their doula develops.) Do you trust her? Do you believe in her competence? Do you feel good in her presence? Trust your instincts.

How do you allow for the opportunity of using a doula? First of all, cost may be a limiting factor for many mothers since most doulas charge $13 to $20 per hour. However, you might consider asking for contributions to a "doula fund" instead of gifts for the baby.

This may afford you the possibility of hiring a doula for the first two to six weeks after the birth and allow you an easier transition. If you can afford a doula's services, you may not need to employ any other caregivers except on a limited basis. Or, if you are fortunate enough to have the support of your family, perhaps a relative could fill in on those occasions when your doula is unavailable.

The National Association of Postpartum Care Services (NAPCS) can provide local referrals for a doula in your area.

General Information:
P.O. Box 1020
Edmonds, WA 98020

Membership Information:
Ellen Hintz, Membership Chair
326 Shields Street
San Francisco, CA 94132

Baby-sitters. Good baby-sitters are hard to find. But once you find a good one, you'll never want to let her go. The search for a baby-sitter can be an arduous task, but, it can also be worth the trouble. Once you find a good match, your baby-sitter can make your life flow much more smoothly. Granted, not all of us require a sitter who is "part of the family." A kind, trustworthy person who can give us a few hours off here and there may fulfill our requirements. Yet, many of us discover we need the assistance of someone we can rely on week in and week out to accommodate work schedules, classes, grocery shopping, and the need for time to pursue our own goals and to nurture our sense of self. But how do we go about finding this person?

Many mothers I spoke with found their baby-sitters by placing classified ads in their local paper. Admittedly, they had to screen a large number of calls and then interview their top candidates, but it usually paid off. One mother told me, "I had to run my ad for three months. Eventually, the perfect match came along. My son loves her, they have a great friendship, and she helps me around the house when he is engaged in his own activities."

To find a good baby-sitter, try asking friends for recommendations. You may want to share a baby-sitter with another mother if you can't afford to hire one full-time. In this situation the baby-sitter might work for you three days a week and for another mother two days a week, for a total of forty hours (or whatever number of hours you all agree on). Another option is to have the baby-sitter watch both families' children at the same time. Not only will this arrangement provide a playmate for your child, but it often reduces the cost of the baby-sitter significantly.

Another woman I know placed an advertisement on Spanish-speaking radio because she wanted a bilingual baby-sitter. Both of her younger daughters were provided with an older sister of sorts by the woman who answered the ad.

Other moms have had success with notices placed at college campuses. Look for bulletin boards in elementary education, childhood psychology, and other related departments where you can post a want ad. You might also consider placing a personal ad in the college newspaper.

The YMCA and YWCA are great resources for finding a babysitter. Not only can you post a notice, but you can speak with the child-care providers on staff (most Ys offer child care for members' children) and find out if they are looking for additional work.

As I have learned in my own experience, it helps to plan ahead. It may take some time for the right person to appear at your door, but with persistence, you will meet someone who works well with your family—someone you can rely on. One mother gave me this advice: "The important thing to remember is, don't wait until you're desperate. You'll make a hasty decision that you might regret. Or, for convenience sake, you'll settle for someone who isn't the best match for your child, and that will make you uneasy about leaving him."

Live-in caregivers. Hiring a live-in nanny is one option for busy mothers who need high-quality child care. Like doulas, these caregivers handle many child-care and household duties. However, their services can be quite expensive, and should it turn out that your child doesn't have an amiable chemistry with the nanny, the situation can be awkward and uncomfortable to terminate. If things do work out, then you will have a caring "second pair of hands" to help keep your life in balance as you strive to be a loving mother. If you are interested in contacting an agency to hire a nanny, call Au Pair in America at (800) 928-7247. Nannies from Europe can be found by calling (800) 479-0907.

Speaking with mothers, I discovered several other child-care arrangements that seemed to be mutually beneficial. One mother traded room and board and a small salary for a certain number of child-care hours each week with the option of additional hours, including full-time care when she had to be out of town. Another mother refinished her basement, giving her three extra bedrooms and a makeshift kitchen, which she rented out to college students at a reduced rate. In exchange for reduced rent, each student agreed to baby-sit her six-year-old daughter as well as prepare meals and do light housekeeping a certain number of hours each month. Two single mothers arranged to share a nanny. It was agreed that the nanny would have a room at each house so she could have a place that was "hers" when she stayed overnight. (Both of these mothers traveled during the week.) The mothers divided the cost of the nanny, and each week a schedule was agreed upon to accommodate everyone's needs. For these single mothers, flexibility was essential. "Both of us do a lot of juggling because our schedules change frequently due to the nature of our work. Thankfully, we found a nanny who is comfortable with a varying routine."

Nanny agencies vary in cost and quality. Many provide emergency nanny services in addition to full- or part-time nannies. If you can find one that will arrange for the same nanny to care for your child as often as possible instead of simply assigning whomever the agency has on hand at the time, then that agency can serve as a reliable backup when your regular child-care provider (baby-sitter, mom, dad) is unable to make it. Unfortunately, these agencies are not always listed in the phone book. You may have to ask around to locate a smaller, family-run service like this.

Mother's helpers. When my son was first born, some of the best daytime help I received was from an eleven-year-old girl named Donna Marie who lived at the end of our block. She came from a tight-knit Italian-Irish family who had recently moved to California after having lived in New York City all their lives. Donna Marie had a strong sense of family and community and was eager to assist me with my new baby. For $2.00

an hour she would entertain Alexander while I napped, show-ered, or typed on the computer. Although she was too young to care for my son without an adult present, I found I could easily take her with me to run errands, and she could tend to Alexander while I shopped. I even took her to a friend's wed-ding so I could have an uninterrupted conversation with the bride and groom (and less drool on my best dress). However, keep in mind that these young helpers, while responsible, are not always capable of handling the same amount of work as a full-fledged baby-sitter. You may have to prepare your child's food or write out detailed directions ahead of time because there are aspects to child care a mother's helper may not be familiar with. Fortunately, you will be nearby should any ques-tions need to be answered.

In my experience, the best age for a mother's helper is nine to twelve years old. About age thirteen fashion and friends tend to distract them, and they become less available after school. Obviously, this varies with the individual, yet it is something to keep in mind.

Perhaps you know a family who has reliable children who would like to help out. Junior high school teachers might be able to suggest a student from one of their classes. You could also speak with members of your church or synagogue. Take some time to acquaint yourself with the mother's helper's fam-ily, especially if they live in your neighborhood; both of you will feel more comfortable. You might discover, as I did, that there are other members of the family who would like to lend a hand. Even if you never take them up on their offers, it is reassuring to know there is help if the need ever arises.

Baby-sitting trades. It is always helpful to have another mother with whom you can trade baby-sitting. Perhaps a close friend is having a baby about the same time as you are, or maybe you've met a mother in your childbirth class who lives nearby.

Discuss an exchange with these mothers. While neither of you may feel ready to care for an additional infant during the first couple of months, keep each others' names (better yet, a list of mothers' names) to call and arrange a trade when life stabilizes a bit. Or, if it seems to be too much to handle two crawling, teething, always-wanting-to-nurse babies at the same time, then look for mothers with children who are slightly older (perhaps six months to a year older) than your child. That way you, and the other mother, will be less likely to be overwhelmed by these baby-sitting trades.

If you decide to create this type of arrangement, remember to keep track of hours so no one feels taken advantage of. And agree that, should one mom be unable to reciprocate, compensation would be made. This is especially important if you plan for this arrangement to be long-standing.

Baby-sitting co-ops. For mothers who choose to stay at home or work part-time, baby-sitting co-ops may be a viable option. Although organizing a co-op can be time consuming at the onset, once the system is up and running smoothly, it won't take any more effort than balancing your checkbook. (Granted, for those of us who may be organizationally impaired, a co-op may not be the way to go.)

There are many ways to run a co-op, and it is important to create an arrangement that works well for all members. Most co-ops have one person keep track of the child-care hours each month on a rotating basis. That person records the number of hours each mother received child care and by whom. She is also the person responsible for activating a phone tree to schedule child care for those mothers who cannot take the time to make numerous phone calls to try to find a baby-sitter.

Of course, certain members may choose to pair up either because their children play well together or the mothers develop a friendship. Yet, as long as these mothers are also available to other members of the group, there should be no problem.

To be a member of a co-op takes a certain level of commitment and the ability to be flexible. Some mothers discover that the co-op works well for their lifestyle, while others may join a co-op for a certain number of months until they find a more permanent method of assistance.

Where does one find a co-op? Many mothers' groups offer a baby-sitting co-op for those members who are interested. Another approach is to start your own. Local parks provide an excellent opportunity to meet other parents who may be interested in joining a co-op in your area. Other mothers have organized neighborhood co-ops by talking with women they have seen out for walks with small children.

Mothers' groups. Mothers' groups that meet on a regular basis either in homes or in parks can provide a lasting support network. Getting together with others who have children around the same age as your child can provide you with a much needed reality check. You can compare notes, swap stories, and laugh at the trials and tribulations of motherhood. And knowing you will be meeting with others in the weeks to come means you'll feel less isolated, because you can count on being in the company of others who are experiencing many of the same things you are. At the same time you will learn about every park and place to picnic within your area and beyond. Some of my favorite parks were introduced to me by my mothers' group, and these spots continue to be a steady source of pleasure for me and my son.

Like baby-sitting co-ops, mothers' groups can be started by anyone. I placed a want ad at the local community center and received an overwhelming response within weeks. Although I led the group initially—typing out schedules, activating the phone tree, writing a newsletter to keep members up-to-date on the changes in each other's lives—I began to delegate more and more responsibilities to the other members as the group became more cohesive. The group disbanded after two years, yet many of us remain close friends.

Another option is to look for ongoing mothers' groups in your area. Some national groups have local branches and draw mothers from a variety of backgrounds. Most of the organization is handled by the local charters so all you have to do is show up. If, on the other hand, you are interested in becoming involved or taking on a leadership role, there are many positions available.

Parents' support. If your parents are like mine—busy professionals who live far away—then counting on grandparents as a steady source of help may be unrealistic. However, if your parents live nearby and are available to baby-sit, don't hesitate to ask them for assistance. Many of my friends have stay-at-home moms who are only too eager to lavish their new grandchildren with love and affection. And since they are pros when it comes to changing diapers, preparing bottles (formula or defrosted breast milk), and drying tears, my friends know their children are in capable hands.

Granted, your mothering style may differ from that of your parents, yet as many mothers told me: "I learned to talk to my folks about the things that were important to me, the rules I wanted them to follow, while simultaneously learning how to trust their methods. Certainly, we had different approaches to child care, but as long as mutual respect prevailed, we struck a balance agreeable to all of us." As the T-shirt reads: "If I'd known how much fun being a grandparent is, I'd have done it first."

Networking, Nurturing, and Numbers

Another aspect to organizing help is gathering all the phone numbers you may need once your baby is born. Remember, the phone is your direct contact to the outside world. It can keep you sane and help you stay connected at a time when you may not be able to leave your house as frequently as you would like. As one mother joked, "The phone is my friend."

- Obstetrician
- Midwife or birth coach
- Postpartum professional (doula, naturopathic physician)
- Health professionals who can help you recover (chiropractor, massage therapist, homeopathic or naturopathic physician)
- Mother's hot line number
- Hospital or birthing center information line number
- Postpartum depression hot line or local contact person
- Pediatrician
- Friends (close friends you can call in an emergency; new mother friends, and single friends who can accompany you on outings, bring dinner over, or stop in after work)
- A neighbor you can rely on in an emergency
- Your partner's work numbers (including pager and car phone)
- A significant other (your partner, your mom, a friend's mom, a college buddy who can fill in especially if you are a single mother)
- Breast-feeding support network: La Leche League International, 800-LA-LECHE (they can also supply a local at-home support person)
- Baby-sitters
- Mother's helpers
- A nanny agency (good source for back-up help if you are able to find a reliable service and you can interview the nannies who would be caring for your child)

- Committee for Quality Birthing: Kathy Weiler, President, P.O. Box 37, Fremont, CA 94537, (510) 429-7075 (advocates for better information, better choices, and better births)
- Birth and Bonding Family Center: 1126 Solano Avenue, Albany CA 94706, (510) 276-9236 (offers practical, educational, emotional support services for the birthing family during preconception, pregnancy, birth, postpartum, and the newborn parenting transition)

Preparing Your Partner for Partnership

During pregnancy most of us focus on ourselves. After all, we are the ones whose body is changing. We feel the subtle movements of a baby inside our body, and then later the thumps and kicks. After all, we read book after book on pregnancy and birth; we buy maternity clothes; and we will bring forth a baby from our body. Enthralled with the miraculous experience of pregnancy, we seldom remember to include our partner in a way that prepares him for becoming a father. We may not have the time or the inclination to assist our partner, especially if we're making motherhood our main responsibility and keeping our partner on the periphery until the last minute. However, preparing our partner—mentally, if not physically—for birth and fatherhood can benefit us and our partner in lasting ways.

Including Dad

One way to involve your partner prior to birth is to have him assist you with the baby's room. For some men, the idea of interior decorating is foreign, and they may feel awkward venturing into this realm. Yet, when couched in terms such as "being the handyman," most fathers-to-be feel more confident of their abilities or more willing to give it a try. A number of fathers I spoke with found that they enjoyed wallpapering, painting, and hanging up pictures. These activities enabled them to prepare for the new arrival in a concrete way. In addition, fixing up the baby's room strengthened their bond with the mother-to-be. They had a mutual focus and, although disagreements occurred, it gave each couple a chance to see how they resolved disputes without much at stake.

Be sure to include your partner in babyproofing your home. Or ask him to be in charge of the project. Again, this is a specific way he can be involved. If you need information on the subject, consult your local library. The information specialists at the reference desk can refer you to a great deal of useful information on the subject.

Another way to include your partner is to have him launder and fold the baby's clothing (blankets, sleepwear, and outer garments should be washed prior to the first use). This will familiarize him with the size of a newborn while bringing closer the reality of a tiny person who will someday fill these clothes.

Encourage your partner to spend time in the baby's room alone, touching clothes and stuffed animals and studying all the gadgets associated with an infant. Then try sitting in the middle of the room together, imagining life-with-baby. Facing each other, look into each other's eyes, hold hands, and talk about your hopes and fears, your expectations and possible disappointments. Take turns rocking in the rocking chair, leaning over the crib, and standing at the changing table. Think about what the baby might look like. Do you have a sense of what your child might be like? Share those thoughts and impressions with each other. Discuss the ways in which you expect your life to change.

Planning for Partnership

Many couples find it helpful to write out an imaginary plan for how a day-in-the-life-with-baby should go. Try it. Chances are, you will discover that your mate's list differs significantly from your own. In fact, how you each picture the day can be very revealing. If, for instance, your partner only sees himself taking care of the baby on weekends, this gives you an opportunity to let him know how your expectations differ. Do you want him to take the baby immediately after work? Is he willing and able to do this every day? If not, you should probably look into hiring help or finding a friend or family member who can provide regularly scheduled relief. On the other hand, are you expecting yourself to meet all of the baby's demands without your partner's assistance, thinking "I can handle it"? If so, you may want to be more realistic. Consider setting aside certain parts of the day for yourself. Can your partner be available in the morning before work? Can he come home for lunch to play with the baby? What if your baby refuses to nap one day (yes, it does happen!)? Do you have a fallback position so you aren't deprived of the rest you need for the day? Since babies take around-the-clock care, be sure to include night schedules in your plans. Who will get up to feed the baby? If you will not be nursing, will you take turns? Or can you arrange to trade off nights? If you are nursing, what about dividing night duty up into feedings and rocking baby back to sleep? Think about it. Many couples come up with a variety of plans to share the night schedule so they are prepared once the baby comes along.

Also, you would be wise to plan for the worst. You must think about things like lack of sleep and sex, intruding relatives, and how you will juggle new and old responsibilities, or else you are in for a rude awakening. Give some thought to how you and your partner will handle certain situations that may arise in the future.

- Who will be responsible for taking time off from work when the baby is sick?
- Who has more flexibility when it comes to altering work schedules?
- Do either of us have the opportunity to rearrange our in-office hours *before* the baby arrives?
- Will it be possible to leave the office and take work home without any penalties?
- What will we do if our child is "high maintenance," requiring more frequent visits to the pediatrician? Who will make these visits?
- What will we do if our baby is colicky or wakeful?
- How will we structure our schedules to accommodate our child's temperament *and* our work schedules?
- Will we feel comfortable with day care? If not, what other options are available and affordable?
- What if one of us chooses *not* to return to work? What kind of lifestyle alterations will we need to make? Are these changes acceptable to both of us?

Take some time to plan. You and your partner may wish to write out Plan A, Plan B, and Plan C to cover as many bases as possible. In all probability you will end up with a combination of these plans (or, if unforeseen circumstances arise, you may have to come up with an entirely new plan). But, even when surprises occur—and be assured, they will—you and your partner will have laid the groundwork for tackling some of the more difficult issues that are part of parenthood. And, by the time baby arrives, you will be in a better position to implement your plans together, as a team.

You may also want to read the chapter, "Striving for True Partnership." If you are already experiencing some of the difficulties listed in this chapter, don't hesitate to seek professional counseling to improve communication and reduce the number of power struggles *before* the baby is born.

Resources:

Books

Haas, Aaron. *The Gift of Fatherhood: How Men's Lives Are Transformed by Their Children.* New York: Fireside, 1994.

Louv, Richard. *Father Love.* New York: Pocket Books, 1993.

Shapiro, Jerrold Lee. *When Men Are Pregnant.* New York: Delta, 1987.

Videotapes

New Fathers, New Lives: A Video to Help Men Make the Transition to Fatherhood. Lifecycle Productions. (617) 964-0047 or (800) 524-1013.

Initiation by Fire

Initiation by fire is the only way to describe my entry into motherhood. While my friends' babies were napping for at least two hours a day, my son refused to be placed in his crib, preferring to catnap at the breast for fifteen-minute intervals throughout the day. I was pinned to the couch by an eight-pound person. When other mothers complained about waking up with their newborns two to three times a night, I envied them. My child was up, wide awake, wailing for milk, five to ten times a night. Just when I thought being a new mother couldn't possibly get to be any more difficult, Alexander began to scream incessantly with some elusive ailment that had no apparent cure: colic. No matter how much I rocked or gently bounced him on my lap, his tears and cries of discomfort continued. To make matters worse, he seemed to be extremely sensitive to sounds and certain kinds of touch. If someone entered the house angry or upset, Alexander would become agitated, and before long he was crying again, even harder than before.

At six weeks old he insisted on being carried a certain way—face forward at adult level—otherwise he'd fuss loudly. Then, at three and a half months, he began to talk: "yes," "hi," and "baby." I was so astonished I called the pediatrician to see if infant vocal chords were actually capable of forming words.

She assured me that Alexander was, as I suspected, talking. As my son grew, he was extremely affectionate and loving, yet he could also become easily frustrated and throw temper tantrums that frightened most adults (not to mention their children). I didn't understand why *my* child seemed so different from everybody else's. On the one hand he asked astonishing questions, was exuberant about life, and engaged in activities with incredible tenacity. But, on the other hand, he was demanding of my attention, unpredictable in his moods, and often impatient. When I spoke with other parents about my experiences they didn't seem to relate to what I was saying. When I sought advice, it rarely worked when I applied it. More often than not, others' methods of parenting had the opposite effect, exacerbating whatever situation I was attempting to improve. Fortunately, I found a book that described my child to the letter and let me know that my experience of motherhood, while universal in many regards, was, indeed, more challenging in some respects: *Raising Your Spirited Child* by Mary Sheedy Kurcinka.

Spirited children, formerly referred to as "difficult children" by most experts, constitute 10 percent to 15 percent of the population and, until recently, were negatively labeled due to their intense, creative, and sometimes explosive temperaments. Ms. Kurcinka defines spirited children in this way: "The word that distinguishes spirited children from other children is *more*. They are normal children who are *more* intense, persistent, sensitive, perceptive, and uncomfortable with change than other children." She goes on to discuss what it is like to be the parent of a spirited child: "Profound statements roll from his mouth, much too mature and intellectual for a child his age. He remembers experiences you've long since forgotten and drags you to the window to watch the raindrops, falling like diamonds from the sky. On the good days being the parent of a spirited child is astounding, dumbfounding, wonderful, funny, interesting, and interspersed with moments of brilliance. The dreadful days are another story. On those days you're not sure you can face another twenty-four hours with him. It's hard to feel good as a parent when you can't even get his socks on, when every word you've said to him is a reprimand, when the innocent act of serving tuna casserole instead of the expected tacos incites a riot, when you realize you've left more public places in a huff with your child in five years than most parents do in a lifetime. You feel weary, drained, and much too old for this. . . ."

How Do You Know If Your Child Is Spirited?

If you are the mother of a spirited or challenging child, chances are you will sense it early on. Most likely, you will notice a difference in your child's emotional intensity. Sometimes you may feel like you are walking on eggshells, trying to avoid doing things that might set your child off. Or on good days you may be awed by your child's enthusiasm and extraordinary energy.

You probably have also noticed others' responses to your child. They don't understand why your child can't behave and sit still like other children. Yet, as Ms. Kurcinka points out: "A child who is temperamentally active not only likes to move but *needs* to move. Telling this child to sit still for extended periods of time, and that he could do it if he really wanted to, is like telling you to ignore a full bladder. . . . Your child's temperament signals a need to act in a particular way—a need that is inside and real."

Because spirited children are so active, because they ask hundreds of probing questions and expect in-depth answers, it is not uncommon to hear mothers of spirited children describe their children as "exhausting," "stubborn," "strong-willed," "demanding," "wild," "unpredictable," and "amazing." Spirited children do take more energy. They demand it. They push the limits, and if we do not take time to rejuvenate ourselves, we quickly burn out, resenting our child's temperament instead of enjoying it.

Mothers of Spirited Children Must Take a Break

- Because spirited children are challenging, their needs can easily eclipse your own.
- Do not compare yourself to other mothers. While this is a good rule of thumb for any mother, it is especially important for mothers of spirited children. You face more challenges on a daily basis than most mothers. This means you are taxed in a number of ways and, like a bank account, you cannot go on making only withdrawals.
- If you feel guilty leaving your spirited child with someone else because your child is so resistant to change and extremely attached to you (and he loudly lets you know his discontent), remember, taking time for yourself will give you the energy needed to better handle the situations that arise with a spirited child. *Both of you* will benefit.

The majority of mothers I spoke with who were raising a spirited child expressed the need for big chunks of free time. As one mother in my "Raising Your Spirited Child" class told me, "I get so frustrated with all of these time-management books that suggest I break up my life into little segments of time. For one thing, it's impossible to go through numerous, quick transitions with a spirited child. Besides, cramming in only ten minutes a day for *me* is just not enough time to regain my balance. I need *at least* a half hour each day, even if it's only driving in the car, and a guarantee that I'll have several hours alone *every* weekend." But, because others often do not understand this need for alone time, many mothers end up feeling guilty about wanting, much less taking, extended periods of time to themselves. As a result, they end up taking little or no time to relax and chastise themselves for not being able to keep up or, worse, think of themselves as completely selfish.

It is essential to remember that, for some, a few minutes a day is the necessary tonic. But, more than likely, especially if you're raising a spirited child, you will fare better if you respect your need for more extended rest periods. Just as books on spirited and challenging children recommend having a flexible attitude about these children and their particular needs, so too must we honor our special needs as the mothers of these energetic and strong-willed individuals.

Create Chunks of Time for Yourself

- Make a schedule and stick to it. Psychologically, if you know a break will be coming, you will be less likely to feel overwhelmed and trapped.
- Ask your partner to give you a half hour in the morning to be alone in bed, read the paper, sip your tea, or sleep.
- Request that your partner, upon returning from work, take your child for a half hour. Even if they only watch a video together, you will have some time to step out of the whirlwind long enough to catch your breath.*
- Plan to have your baby-sitter stay for an extra hour in the evening one or two times a week so both you and your partner can take a half hour to wind down in the car on the way home.
- Arrange for someone other than your partner to take your

---

*While spirited children tend to be very energetic, they should not be confused with hyperactive children or children with Attention Deficit Disorder (ADD). The difference is in a child's ability to focus on a subject or project. Occasionally, spirited children will be easily distracted, but they also possess an incredible ability to focus and even "lock in." Hyperactive children and those with ADD often have difficulty keeping their attention on any one thing or person.

child out to play for several hours every weekend. Remember, spirited children generally enjoy bouncing off of other people.

- Put your child to bed at a "decent hour, starting at an early age." Remember, if you want your spirited child asleep by 8:30, start winding down with a bath and a book at 7:00. If your spirited child is having trouble sleeping (which is often the case), please read Ms. Kurcinka's chapter on bedtime and night waking. Most other books on sleep problems create more problems than they solve because "crying it out" can produce so much stress that a spirited child becomes too upset to settle down. Thus, you end up with less sleep instead of more.

A Plan for "Catching Up"

Along with implementing a regular schedule that accommodates your needs (as well as your partner's), it is often helpful to devise a plan for "catching up." As I discovered in my spirited child class, most mothers had been hanging in there, hoping for change instead of creating it. We were sure a time would come when our child would be over this phase, and we could resume a normal life. When all of us finally realized that this was the way our child was going to be, we decided not to wait until he left for college before we took some time to ourselves.

- Allow yourself to collapse. Plan a weekend to yourself. Go to a retreat center so you will not be tempted to answer the phone, fold socks, or prepare meals for the upcoming week. Retreat centers are inexpensive, and they usually provide cooked meals, trails for hiking, spas, and a non-invasive atmosphere (for more information, see the chapter "Sanctuaries").
- Hire a helper for several hours each day. Not only can she assist your mate with household chores (less guilt for you,

less potential resentment from your mate), but she can have things ready when you return so you won't have to "catch up" from "catching up"!

- Plan to get a massage or facial or to take a hot bath on your first day away from home. This will make it easier to relax. You may find it difficult to unwind and release the tension that has built up without some assistance.
- Once you shift gears, you may find that all you want to do is sleep. Go ahead! Your body *and your mind* may be starved for uninterrupted sleep.
- Suspend all schedules. While it is tempting to want to turn your attention to the many things you've put on hold, pace yourself. The goal for this weekend is to begin to regenerate your body, mind, and spirit.
- When your body is relaxed, emotions you've been harboring may rise to the surface. You may feel alone in your experience of motherhood, resentful that your child is "different," angry that life with your child seems so much harder. You may also feel compassion for the fact that you've had to "feel your way in the dark," and relief that you were right—your situation was not the same as others.
- All of these feelings are common among mothers of spirited children. Allow yourself to feel them! They can serve as catalysts for greater understanding of your child and yourself. Indeed, they can help you gain perspective of your particular situation and motivate you to reorganize your life in a way that is more respectful of your family's needs and different temperaments.
- Plan to take a weekend every month for a few months until you feel your energy stabilizing or as often as your budget and circumstances will allow. And don't forget the necessary maintenance during the week. Eventually, you will notice that life with a spirited child is running more smoothly

because you are more patient and less prone to take their behavior personally.

- I highly recommend reading and implementing the strategies provided by the books listed in this chapter. They will change your perspective and give you effective tools. In addition, contact the YMCA, YWCA, community colleges, and local hospitals and birthing centers to find out if they offer a spirited or challenging child class. Hearing other mothers verbalize similar experiences while learning to maximize your child's gifts will renew your commitment to motherhood. Many classes form their own support groups, and the advice and suggestions from other mothers is invaluable.

Resources:

Forehand, Rex, and Nicholas Long. *Parenting the Strong-Willed Child*. Chicago: Contemporary Books, 1996.

Golant, Mitch, and Donna G. Corwin. *The Challenging Child: A Guide for Parents of Exceptionally Strong-Willed Children*. New York: Berkeley Books, 1995.

Greenspan, Stanley I. *The Challenging Child: Understanding, Raising and Enjoying the Five "Difficult" Types of Children*. Menlo Park, CA: Addison Wesley, 1995.

Kurcinka, Mary Sheedy. *Raising Your Spirited Child*. New York: HarperCollins, 1991.

Healing Childbirth Trauma

Today, more than ever, a woman who gives birth in a hospital is likely to undergo some form of medical intervention whether it be a cesarean delivery, episiotomy, fetal monitoring, or the administering of pharmaceutical drugs. As a result, an increasing number of women are facing invasive medical procedures that traumatize the birthing mother, sometimes leaving a scar on her belly, but even more often on her psyche. Of course, not all mothers experience the trauma of surgery and complicated births when medical intervention is used as an invasive process—some breeze through the birth experience relatively unharmed. Yet, because the numbers of women who have experienced trauma at childbirth are on the rise and the commonality of their stories is just recently being recognized as a "legitimate" psychological phenomenon needing to be addressed, I've included this section as an important aspect of healing after birth.

Granted, you may not have the time or energy to focus on this ritual during the first few months after your baby arrives. Trust your own timing. You may want to come back to it when life-with-baby stabilizes and you feel ready to embrace the pain, grief, and vulnerability that often accompany surgery and other invasive procedures. Pay attention to the wisdom of your body.

35

It will let you know when you are strong enough to handle the emotional release of the past. For instance, if you find yourself constantly talking about the birth, relating the details over and over to anyone who asks, please begin the healing process right away by getting support from the International Cesarean Awareness Network listed at the end of this section. I also recommend talking with your doctor or a therapist.* Otherwise, you may perpetuate feelings of failure, inadequacy, and grief, and these could eventually cause you to feel alienated from your baby. In addition, if your infant was bruised or mildly injured during birth due to medical intervention, it is highly likely that you will feel responsible and at fault. Speak with someone who has gone through a similar ordeal. It will ease your mind and you will feel less alone.

Write Down Your Feelings

If you have experienced a particularly difficult birth, chances are your movement will be slightly restricted for a short time (and if you've had a cesarean section, you may need to take it easy for several weeks or even several months). Take advantage of the fact that you're couch-bound. Have your partner or a member of your support team buy a notebook for you if you don't already have a journal. Most grocery stores carry them nowadays. Then, place your notebook at your nursing station or bedside. While your baby naps, take a few moments to write down your perceptions of the birth.

First, write down what happened. Write out your account of the details. Details are important. Details are meaningful. They help us hold our place within a chaotic and out-of-control situation—even after the fact. They are the markers

---

*Naturopaths and homeopaths can also provide good emotional and physical support.

that tell us over and over, "You are here." And they bring the past to life so we can remember it and, eventually, let it go.

When I had an emergency cesarean section everyone around me was moving quickly, but from my vantage point, time moved slowly and I was able to absorb an astonishing number of details: the color of the nurse's lipstick, expressions on people's faces, the smell of the operating room, the touch of my mother's hand, the sound of my mother's voice standing up for me during a confrontation with a quarrelsome medical assistant. I could feel the fear in the room, others' fear as well as my own, and I could feel my son inside of me, ready to come out. My mind was spinning with millions of thoughts. I was experiencing so much at once and, as I later discovered through writing, I had been overwhelmed, yet highly cognizant of the entire event. Recording the details helped to make the experience more real; they brought it out in the open so I wouldn't have to hold the intensity of it all inside of me.

Next, write down what you learned during the experience. Often, by recording the details of your feelings during the birth process and of the procedures themselves and their effect on you, you will discover options you may have had but were not aware of at the time. You may think of questions you wanted to ask, but were afraid to ask because you were placing your confidence in your physician or midwife. Writing these down will enable you to seek answers for any unanswered questions, to educate yourself so you can make more informed decisions in the future, and to empower yourself by coming to understand all the things you and your partner did right, especially in cases where none of the options seemed like good options.

Now, write down what you wished would have happened. Write down the birth experience you would have wanted. If you already wrote out what you imagined to be the perfect birth during pregnancy, compare it to your idea of the perfect birth now, knowing what you know. What ideas still appeal to you? Which aspects now seem unrealistic under the circumstances? Do you still think you could have had a more perfect birth if only a nurse or a doctor or a birthing coach had done something differently?

As you write, allow yourself to feel your disappointment, loss, and grief. Allow yourself to feel angry and hurt. Allow yourself to feel the bittersweet realities of life—you experienced the miracle of birth amid crisis and uncertainty. Allow yourself to feel the intense vulnerability inherent in being a mother: you could have taken care of yourself, but you may have felt powerless to help your baby. If you need to ask why things didn't turn out the way you wanted them to, then ask, on paper. If you feel like things went wrong, write out what you think went wrong. Don't think about what you're writing, just let the words flow. Don't judge.

Then, in a couple of hours or perhaps the next day, look at what you've put down. Do you see a lot of self-blame? Are you beating yourself up? Are you feeling as though you failed and you're worthless because you didn't have "the right kind of birth"? Do you feel guilty? Deep down do you believe it will affect your relationship with your child? If so, then take some time to write a letter to yourself using the same voice you would use to speak to your baby. You wouldn't tell your baby that being born a certain way was wrong, would you? You wouldn't fault your baby for doing what she thought was best for the moment during a difficult situation. You would not castigate your child for not knowing exactly what to do.

Spend some time forgiving yourself, and if you can't seem to get past your anger and tears, ask someone to be with you while you read what you've written about the birth. The compassion of others may help you to find more self-compassion.

Eventually, you might want to write down a brief paragraph that brings you into the present. For example: "I am a mother now. My child is six months old and is learning new things everyday. When I am nursing, and I look into my baby's eyes and see such content love, I am overwhelmed. I am tired. I think about returning to work. What will it be like after these months at home?"

Pay attention to what is going on today, at this very moment.

Releasing Ritual

Purpose:

To Heal the Pain of Childbirth Trauma by Releasing the Experience from Our Body, Mind, and Spirit.

Ask a friend to fix up a room in your house to be used as a healing space. (It does not need to be elaborate.) Decorate it with flowers and candles. You may wish to play some soothing background music that invokes a sense of serenity.

Place a foam pad on the floor. Have your closest friends sit around the pad, creating a safe container for the expression of your emotions. Only invite those close friends whom you feel you can confide in and share your deeper feelings.

Have each person place a hand on part of your body. For example, one person might place a hand over your heart, another might lightly touch your forehead, while another might hold a hand on your belly. Let each person, in turn, acknowledge the miracle your body has performed by listening, with an intuitive ear, to the messages being conveyed by your body. In other words, the friend whose hand is resting on your heart might feel the sadness and grief in your heart—perhaps disappointment about the way your baby entered the world and sadness about how your body was treated. And your friend may also feel the happiness and joy you hold in your heart. Let her tell you what messages she feels are being conveyed by your body. (If your friend can't seem to find the words, or feels awkward, afraid she might not be "attuned" enough to hear the "right" messages, ask her to simply hold her hand over your heart.) The purpose of this part of the ritual is not to analyze or interpret but to give a thoughtful gift of acknowledgment, from close friends, of what you went through during delivery and the impact it had on you and your baby. Words such as, "It must have hurt your heart to hear your baby crying and not be able to do anything to help. I know how much you love your child; your heart is full of love," carry a lot of healing power. The relief of knowing that someone understands what you endured during childbirth (one of the most vulnerable moments in your life) is also incredibly healing.

Next, after everyone has taken a turn, have one of your friends sing a soothing song or perhaps a lullaby. Then have another friend read what you've written about your memories of the birth and how you felt during the labor and delivery.

Allow your feelings to emerge, and listen to the wisdom of your tears, laughter, anger, and sorrow. Be sure to allow for the time you need to run the gamut of your feelings. If you need to be held, ask one of your friends to hold you. You may also want to be rocked or cradled in someone's arms. This ritual can be an intense catharsis or a quiet healing. Trust it to give you what you need.

Gentle Measures for Healing After a Cesarean Section

Cesarean sections vary from woman to woman. For some, the surgery is minor. Others experience the entire event as devastating. In the latter case, a woman can feel abused, battered, and violated at a time when what she needed most was to feel loved, supported, and comforted.

After the initial trauma is over, a tender scar on the belly serves as a reminder. While it is tempting to ignore the incision once the stitches are removed, it is essential not to. Our body needs attention and tender loving care. We need to act as witnesses to the pain endured and the fear felt and to embrace these as part of us instead of distancing ourselves in an attempt to cope. Many of us who ended up having a cesarean section, especially an emergency or unanticipated cesarean section, tend to feel disassociated from our body for a time. This is normal, but it should not go on indefinitely.

To begin giving your body the attention it needs, try standing in front of a mirror. Take a few moments to look at your scar. Introduce yourself to it by gently running your fingers over the length of it. Go slowly if you begin to feel squeamish, nauseated, or exposed. Then take a vitamin E capsule and pierce it open with a needle. Lie down and apply the vitamin liquid to your incision, gently rubbing it in. If this is too messy, you may want to buy some vitamin E cream at your local health-food store. Be sure it contains 25,000 IU of vitamin E. This cream will help your skin heal more quickly, and your scar won't be so tender. If possible, apply vitamin E every day. You may want to ask your partner to apply it for you in the evening before bed so you'll be less concerned about getting it on your clothes, although vitamin E cream won't stain most fabrics. Make sure your partner is attentive to what he is doing. Touching a cesarean section incision, applying cream to it, is not the same as putting on suntan lotion at the beach. Your body has been through major surgery and needs special care. Treat it as such.

When you feel ready, stroke the entire area surrounding your incision. Cradle your scar in the palm of your hand. Close your eyes. Say a quiet prayer of thanks to your body. Be aware of all your body has accomplished by bringing your baby into the world.

Months later, when your incision no longer feels uncomfortable, you may want to use a gentle skin brush directly on it. By using light, circular strokes, you will bring the blood to the surface of the skin and at the same time soften the scar tissue and make it more elastic. In this way, you won't feel so much pulling when you lift your baby, exercise, or make love. Also, the natural shape of your belly will return more quickly. You may want to try bringing your skin brush in the bath or shower with you. The water on the bristles can prevent them from being too stiff and coarse on your skin.

Again, as you brush, thank your body for giving birth. Take a moment to feel grateful for its recovery.

Resources:
International Cesarean Awareness Network (ICAN)
1304 Kingsdale Avenue
Redondo Beach, CA 90278
(310) 542-6400

Books

Cohen, Nancy Wainer. *Silent Knife.* South Hadley, MA: Bergin & Garvey, 1983.

Odent, Michel, M.D. *Birth Reborn.* Medford, NJ: Birthworks, 1994.

Rothman, Barbara Katz. *In Labor: Women and Power in the Birthplace.* New York: W. W. Norton & Company, 1991.

Striving for True Partnership

Undoubtedly, a baby places demands on both parents. Yet, as I've listened to mothers talk, I have noticed a recurring theme: many mothers feel they are taking on more than their share of raising the children and performing household responsibilities, and they are often frustrated by this inequity. Over and over I hear mothers ask, "How can I get my partner to take a more active role in bringing up our children?" "How can I get him to participate more at home?" Ironically, when I begin to address their concerns, many of these mothers withdraw as if they're worried they've said something wrong and they should take it back. How could they have maligned their partner in this way? "He is a good father," they insist as if to make up for their earlier comments. "He tries," they tell me, assuming I must envision him as nothing more than a football-watching couch potato. "I guess he's doing the best he can," I hear with a sigh of resignation.

The truth is, most of us have trouble admitting that we have a sometimes unsupportive partner who may need some improvement in the domestic arena. But why do we feel so guilty? Would we feel this guilt if we said that our partner needed to learn more about a recently released computer software program? Or any other new thing for that matter? Of course not. Then why? Although the reallocation of work in the home is no longer thought of as unusual, caring for children continues to be thought of as primarily "women's work." These subtle messages perpetuate the feelings of guilt in mothers when we ask our spouse to take on a more active role. To ask our partner to do his share would seem unreasonable. Perhaps we are afraid of hurting his feelings or alienating him. Or, maybe, the thought of having an unsupportive partner is too frightening. With a task as daunting as caring for a child, it makes us feel all alone, and so we minimize our feelings and try harder to cope.

The fact is, if our mate is not contributing in meaningful ways, we are more susceptible to burnout. According to a ten-year study conducted by Carolyn Pape Cowan and Philip A. Cowan, mothers who have children under the age of five and who do not have a supportive partner are at a greater risk for becoming clinically depressed than any other group of adults. Since we are virtually "doing the job of two," it is much more difficult to keep up with demands. As a result, our confidence is sabotaged, we feel extremely alienated, our self-worth takes a beating, and if conditions do not improve, eventually, our relationships will suffer. Instead of bringing us closer together, becoming parents has the opposite effect: alienation, resentment, anger, and disappointment. Fortunately, many men are striving to be caring fathers. They want to be involved. They want to be supportive. They just don't know how.

Resistance vs. Apprentice-in-Training

It is important to pay attention to your partner's actions in order to determine whether he is purposely resisting participation in childrearing and domestic chores, or if he is not actively giving support simply because he isn't sure how to approach the new challenges that confront him as a father.

- Does he verbally reassure you that he wants to support you and the baby, but when you ask for assistance, concrete help rarely materializes?
- When at home, does he "hide-out" in the bathroom or elsewhere in the house for inordinate amounts of time?
- When you give him explicit directions for small tasks such as preparing a bottle or putting the baby down to nap, does he scramble to find something "more important" to occupy his time?
- When you ask for his help, does he use your request as an excuse to argue, making you feel somehow at fault for asking him to contribute?
- Does he avoid coming home, working later and later hours?
- Does he seem unwilling to talk about the division of household duties, as if these matters are already settled and there's no reason to change unspoken agreements?
- Does he promise to tend to certain chores or to take the baby for certain periods of time, but then doesn't follow through?
- When you tell him you're feeling overwhelmed and overburdened does he refuse to offer his help and instead insist that it is your job to find outside help (e.g., "Can't your mother watch the baby?").
- Do you find yourself striving to keep your spouse's life "normal," trying to prevent the baby from disturbing him since *he is the one who works*?
- Is your work (inside and outside the home) discounted in subtle and not-so-subtle ways?
- Does he criticize the way in which you care for the baby, but fail to offer alternative suggestions or assistance?

If you answered "yes" to two or more of these questions, then chances are your partner is actively resisting participation. There could be many reasons for this type of behavior. Yet, if he refuses to acknowledge that any changes need to be made, and he is reluctant to work toward any resolution, you may want to get professional assistance. Perhaps, with the help of a third party, you can begin to examine and possibly change the roles each of you has taken on in your relationship and move toward an arrangement that is more aggreeable and satisfying to both of you.* Also, you would be afforded the opportunity of developing better communication skills and tools for resolving conflict—a definite asset for parents *and* spouses.

If, on the other hand, your partner simply doesn't know how to approach daddyhood, that is another matter entirely. He wants to learn, he wants to care for your child, he just isn't sure how to go about it. He needs guidance. He needs tools. He needs detailed instructions until he can get the hang of it.

It is important to remember that just because he is eager to learn doesn't mean that he won't be defensive and hostile at times. Like you, he will not always greet the responsibilities of parenthood with unadulterated cheerfulness. He will experience many of the same feelings you do: inadequacy, impatience (with himself and the baby), frustration, exasperation, giddiness, self-consciousness (especially if he feels you are monitoring him), intense love (which, for many men, may not be easy to express), protectiveness (of you and the baby), helplessness, abundant joy, and financially pressured.

And Baby Makes Three

For many men, thinking of parenting as a team effort is a concept they can readily understand. You might begin by show-

---

*Statistically, the rate of divorce for parents increases significantly around their child's second birthday. This owes largely to a lack of support from a woman's partner and a refusal to change the status quo. If you find yourself experiencing the types of problems listed, please contact a counselor or therapist who can give you emotional support and help you and your partner function more effectively as a couple.

ing your partner how certain basics are handled (and because you're just learning yourself, you might join forces to see if you can figure out the best approach together—learning to use a breast-pump is a case in point).

- Show him how to change a baby's diaper. (Don't assume he knows where or how to dispose of it, where extras are stored, etc.) Provide every step. If he becomes overwhelmed by verbal instructions, write them down.
- Show him how to dress and undress the baby.
- Let him help you bathe the baby.
- If you have found ways your infant likes to be held or rocked, share them with your mate. Also, encourage him to experiment with his own methods, especially when your baby is crying. He may discover new techniques to expand your repertoire.
- Take him through the steps of taking the baby for a walk in the stroller: putting on baby's hat, applying sunscreen, and showing him how to fold up the stroller (quite a challenge for most of us!). Tell him what to include in the diaper bag.
- Have him prepare the baby's bottle or defrost expressed milk and put it into a sterilized bottle to feed the baby. (You may have to leave the room so your infant doesn't see or smell you. Otherwise, the baby may refuse the feeding from your partner.)
- In the evening, show him the routine you've developed: rocking the baby, singing lullabyes, massaging baby's feet, softly stroking baby's head, etc. Then he can put baby to sleep while you wash your face, brush your teeth, and change into your nightgown (these are luxuries in the first few months).
- Give him a basket full of toys to entertain the baby; show him how to use the automatic swing; pull out the gadgets that dangle from the bar over the baby carrier. Then leave him to his own devices. You may be amazed by what he finds to entertain the baby.

Things to Keep in Mind

- If your partner seems reluctant to learn from you, or your instructions seem to be the precursor for too many power struggles, suggest that he register for a parenting class. Or, if you are already enrolled in one, ask your partner to join you for several sessions. Many hospitals, community colleges, and continuing education programs at universities offer parenting classes. See what's available.

- Write out lists for your partner. I used to think this was demeaning, but my partner appreciates it. And it works! Jim says, "You wouldn't expect a professor *not* to hand out a syllabus on the first day of class, would you?" Certainly not. So, try it. Your partner will know what is expected of him, and he will be better prepared. In addition, there may be aspects to caring for a child that he simply doesn't know about. Your list will inform him. Be sure to prioritize your list and don't expect everything to be done perfectly the first (or second) time around. It may take a few months for him to learn to incorporate these details into his former routine. Sound familiar? Also, it would be helpful to let him know that the list is not written in stone. As you both will discover, the list will need to be altered as your child's needs change. (Don't forget to tailor the list to your needs as well.)

- If there's a parenting problem you want to discuss, try to avoid shouting it out in the middle of the event. (Of course this will happen sometimes, but try not to make a habit of it. Otherwise, you will end up working against each other.) If you don't agree on a certain approach to parenting, try coming up with a compromise that is comfortable for both of you. The best time to discuss these potentially "touchy" subjects is when you have a quiet moment alone. Admittedly, these are not easy to find, but do the best you can.

- Let your partner know you appreciate him. Let him know you love him. Encourage his efforts and, if he isn't reciprocating, ask him to applaud you for all you've been handling. Mutual support, love, and recognition is essential! You'll be getting enough advice and criticism from plenty of other people, including total strangers! Why compound the problem?

- Let your partner know that sometimes you simply need to vent your feelings, and he need not take them personally or provide answers and solutions. Many men don't realize that one of the best things they can do for you is to listen to you and hold you in their arms. Explain to your partner that simply "being present" is often the most affirming and loving support he can give. Many men—and some women, for that matter—don't understand what it means to be present for someone else. You may ask your partner to try some of the exercises in the "Sex and Intimacy" chapter.

Gloria Steinem once said: "I have yet to hear a man say that he is struggling to balance work and family." Fortunately, things are changing. Many men are taking on more of the responsibilities involved in raising a family. And, undoubtedly, they, too, are experiencing the stresses and strains of keeping so many balls in the air at once. Certainly, being on the front line of child-rearing is the toughest job you'll ever love (although you won't like it every day!). As one mother of two said to me: "Motherhood is not for wimps!" Neither is fatherhood. In a true partnership, there is mutual respect and support. Both of you, no matter how hectic life gets, contribute. And you'll find there is nothing more satisfying, nor more strengthening in a relationship, than working together and cooperating—that way both of you get to share in the infinite joys and challenges of parenthood.

Resources:

Ammer, Christine, with Nathan Sidley, M.D. *Getting Help: A Consumer's Guide to Therapy.* New York: Paragon House, 1991.

Berry, Mary Frances. *The Politics of Parenthood.* New York: Penguin Books, 1993.

Carter, Steven, and Julia Sokol. *Men Like Women Who Like Themselves (and Other Secrets that the Smartest Women Know).* New York: Delacorte Press, 1996.

Cowan, Carolyn Pape, and Philip A. Cowan. *When Partners Become Parents: The Big Life Change for Couples.* New York: BasicBooks, 1992.

Epstein, Rick. *Rookie Dad.* New York: Hyperion, 1992.

Hochschild, Arlie. *The Second Shift.* New York: Avon Books, 1989.

Sachs, Brad E. *Things Have Never Been the Same.* New York: William Morrow, 1992.

Waring, Marilyn. *If Women Counted.* San Francisco, CA: HarperCollins, 1988.

Postpartum Depression

Whidle the time following birth is magical, filled with awe and wonder, there is another aspect to it, one that is often overlooked by family, friends, and even "the experts," namely: postpartum depression (PPD). Hormone levels are changing dramatically. In her article "Postpartum Depression," Martha Leathe indicates that "prior to childbirth, levels of progesterone and estrogen are as much as 50 percent higher than usual, and within hours after childbirth they fall to below normal levels." As a result, we are susceptible to intense feelings of disorientation, anxiety, fear, depression, sadness, and guilt. Although the severity of postpartum depression varies with each individual, most of us experience, to one degree or another, feelings of inadequacy when trying to meet our babies' needs, lack of confidence, fatigue and loss of energy due to breast-feeding, sleep deprivation (used as a torture throughout the world!), feelings of isolation and separation from the "outside world," physical discomfort, and debilitating exhaustion. In addition, we may feel overwhelmed by the new demands of motherhood, and it may take a while to achieve some balance in our lives. Even for mothers who have experienced it before, PPD often comes as a terrifying surprise.

Do not be afraid to seek help and ask for assistance. You

are not alone. Postpartum depression is very common and can be relieved in a variety of ways—through diet, exercise, stress-reduction, homeopathic remedies, vitamins, and, if necessary, medication.

The Blues

Most of us have had some experience with "the blues." While pregnant we wept over sentimental commercials and sobbed during the ending of a heart-wrenching movie. Even a gorgeous sunset gave us cause for tears. Now that we are mothers, our hormones are acting to regulate various functions within our body: shrinking our uterus back to normal size, producing milk to feed our baby, and tightening ligaments to name just a few. Owing to fluctuations in hormone levels, the majority of postpartum mothers will have bouts of "the blues" during the first two weeks to twelve months after birth. We will feel like crying at the slightest provocation, we will take far too many comments personally, and we will whine about the challenges of motherhood, sometimes wanting to be mothered ourselves. *All of these feelings are normal.* Don't discount how sensitive you feel. As one of my closest friends commented, "Now that I have a baby, I'm much more sensitive, highly sensitive, as if God had intended me to experience everything a newborn experiences."

Another common experience is to feel moody. One minute we're ecstatic, feeling totally blissful about our little angel sent from the ethers, then the next minute we're plotting our escape from the horrors of suburbia, afraid we might turn into one of the Stepford wives. Again, *mood swings are normal.* It is common to feel reactive, easily insulted, insecure, slothful, edgy, irrational, angry, lonely, irritable, intensely loving, spaced out, and a bit disoriented—all within the same day or even the same hour! Certainly, early motherhood is an unforgettable emotional roller-coaster ride.

Other Common Early Motherhood Experiences Associated with the Blues

Longing for life-before-baby. No, this does not mean your child is unwanted. This is a natural part of the grieving cycle as you come to terms with the monumental changes in your life. As I always tell new mothers, "This is the toughest job you'll ever love. It doesn't mean you'll always feel thrilled about it. There will be plenty of times you'll look back nostalgically, amazed at how comparatively simple life was b.c. (before child)."

Experiencing grief and a sense of loss. Loss of your former self, loss of your freedom, and loss of alone time with your mate can make you sad. This is normal. It does not mean you made a mistake in becoming a mother. Be gentle with yourself.

Noticing emergence of feelings and vivid memories of your own past, particularly your own childhood. Any resentments you harbor toward your parents may arise as well as happy memories you may long to duplicate or relive. It helps to write down the feelings and memories you are now reexperiencing as a result of becoming a mother yourself. If you feel it would help, find a counselor who can guide you as you sort through your past.

Experiencing intense and irrational fear. You may feel more fragile and vulnerable than you ever have in your life, rushing to the nursery whenever you cannot hear the baby breathing, feeling sure that a mild cold is going to turn into a life-threatening illness, fearing the worst if your partner arrives home late.

Ask for reassurance from your partner, your friends, your family. Ask for a hug, or lots of hugs and holding to quell your fears and make you feel more secure. Try not to judge yourself or castigate yourself for "being weak" and "neurotic." Feeling the weight of responsibility for another human being, one you love so deeply, can temporarily overwhelm your senses.

Envisioning, in graphic detail, violent episodes. A dog suddenly attacking your child, a stranger torturing your child and you are helpless to stop him, or other "blood and guts" scenes not unlike the movies—these are not uncommon thoughts or dreams during the emotional period that follows childbirth.

Feeling you hate your baby. As vile as this seems, it is normal, and it happens to most mothers, especially when you are not getting enough sleep, your baby won't stop crying, and you are at your wits' end rocking and cajoling your infant. You feel sure your child is wailing on purpose in an attempt to drive you crazy. At times like these, it is essential to take a break. Set your child down in his crib even if he is still crying and ask someone else to tend to him for thirty minutes—or, if you can arrange it, for a few hours.

Feeling helpless and out-of-control. There is nothing more maddening than to discover that no matter how hard you try, you cannot always soothe your infant or that you cannot always automatically decipher what is the best course of action in a given situation. Try as you might, you cannot always take away your baby's discomfort, and you cannot always "make things better." Not only is this a humbling experience, but it can make us feel helpless, frightened, and inadequately equipped to handle motherhood. Before you jump to any conclusions about your performance, call your midwife, pick up a parenting magazine, or phone a hospital information line to learn about how universal your experience is.

Feeling confused, lethargic (mentally and physically), disoriented, and spaced out. Sleep deprivation has a lot to do with these emotional and psychological states. If you begin to feel as though you are always removed from the present, however, seek outside help and demand time for uninterrupted sleep to pull yourself back from the abyss.

Feeling as if you are not functioning normally and that every other mother is having an easier time adjusting to motherhood. Thankfully, most mothers handle their new lives just fine. But you may feel especially overwhelmed if you have set your expectations too high. Talk to other mothers, talk to your partner, or talk to your doctor or midwife to gain a more balanced perspective. You may also want to read my first book: *Meditations for New Mothers*.

Experiencing forgetfulness. As one mother confided: "I feel as if my brain came out with the afterbirth!" It is normal to lose your memory when you first become a mother. Not only are there physiological reasons for this, but you may be overwhelmed by the extraordinary number of details you must incorporate into your life. This factor alone can cause mental exhaustion and chronic forgetfulness (and can easily be worsened by lack of sleep).

Feeling elation, bliss, and ecstacy. You may have an unprecedented number of transpersonal experiences where you feel filled with intense angelic or otherworldly love, you enter altered states of consciousness, and you are tempted to join a mystical spiritual order. Don't worry. This is normal. The mir-

acle of childbirth and the depth of human love are upon you—
enjoy!

Experiencing separation anxiety. Leaving your infant with
other people can be difficult. Initially, it may create too much
anxiety for you, especially if the person with whom you are
leaving your baby is not a close friend or someone you have
had the opportunity to develop trust in. Be patient with yourself. The first few months are an intense time of merging and
bonding for both mothers and their infants. It will feel strange
and scary to not always be with your baby. The best remedy is
to practice leaving your infant with your partner or a reliable
friend while you read or rest in another part of the house (try
to resist interfering if your baby cries). Then, when you feel
ready, ask the same person to care for your infant while you
go out for a couple of hours (be sure to leave a phone number where you can be reached in an emergency—this will ease
your mind). Gradually, you will feel less anxiety and more confidence that it's all right for you *and baby* to be away from each
other for certain periods of time.

If your infant is prone to prolonged crying due to colic or
extreme sensitivity and exhibits anxiety whenever someone
other than you holds her, it is imperative that you find someone whom you truly trust to care for your child. That way,
you can be confident that your friend won't leave your child
in her crib "to cry it out" without comforting her. In addition, you will feel more comfortable with separation if you can
speak frankly about your own needs and expectations (and be
taken seriously instead of being treated as if your needs are
"silly" or "unreasonable"), knowing your sitter will attend lovingly to your child's individual needs.

Also, believe it or not, I discovered that whenever I could

strongly envision my heart joined with my son's, I always received glowing reports about how little he cried during my absence. You might try it. Or create your own visualization.

Feeling dumpy and dull. The fact that you've just had a baby, that you've just performed a miracle, that your extra weight has a purpose, seems to instantly escape your mind once your baby is in your arms. As a product of a society obsessed with weight control and prolonged, upbeat happiness, it is no wonder you feel this way. However, before you rush to the gym, spend a little time thanking your body and seeing its innate beauty. Go to the library and borrow books filled with pictures of voluptuous women. Return to the "Bonding with Baby" chapter and take a few moments to remember, with your fingertips, how perfect you and your baby are.

Beyond the Blues: Postpartum Depression (PPD)

While it is common for all new mothers to experience a range of emotions in a short span of time, postpartum depression is an amplification of these emotions. In fact, the emotions a mother experiences—fear, anxiety, severe disassociation, anger, and guilt—often become so intense that she feels completely out-of-control. She may start to believe she is losing her sanity. And this, of course, creates more fear and anxiety, more anger and guilt at a very vulnerable time. That is why it is imperative for a mother to seek and receive help. Otherwise, a downward cycle will ensue, making it almost impossible to function much less care for a newborn baby. Remember: postpartum depression is 100 percent treatable. If you suspect you have postpartum depression or are on the verge of having it, by all means call for outside assistance.

Warning Signals

Feeling grief and loss. If you feel the kind of debilitating grief that is most often associated with the death of a loved one, and you can't seem to "get out from under it," you need outside support.

Feeling out of touch with reality. If you feel out of touch with reality, disassociated from the present (as though you are watching events, but are not part of them), and have a vague sense of being removed from your life, seek help.

Fearing hurting your baby. If the thoughts of handling your baby, giving her a bath, or leaving her in her crib create anxiety or a fear that your actions will cause harm to your child, call someone who can assist you with PPD.

Having horrible thoughts and hearing internal voices. If you begin to have thoughts about hurting your baby or yourself (or feel as if a foreign voice inside of you is giving you instructions), call one of the organizations listed at the end of the chapter immediately.

Feeling disoriented. If you feel as though you can't remember who you are, if you become lost while out on familiar streets, or if you are fearful of always forgetting your baby or leaving him somewhere, please reach out for help.

Having difficulty making decisions. If you are reading this list of warning signals with mounting anxiety, unable to decide whether you really have PPD or are simply "having a hard time," or if all choices feel like life-or-death decisions that you are too anxious and overwhelmed to make, seek outside support right away.

Feeling despondent and overwhelmed. If you feel your life has been reduced to pure survival and you're so overwhelmed that you can't even will yourself to attend to any or all of the details of life—every chore, every change of a diaper, drains you and creates resentment day after day—make a phone call to one of the organizations listed.

Experiencing nervous exhaustion. If you feel exhausted, yet nervous and anxious at the same time (chances are your adrenal system is totally overtaxed), and if you are having trouble sleeping and relaxing even when baby is sleeping, you may be on your way to a full-blown case of PPD. Seek outside help not only for emotional support, but to counter the effects of physical burnout.

I strongly recommend getting assistance from health-care professionals who have been highly successful with PPD: chiropractors, massage therapists, and naturopathic and homeopathic physicians. Also, request a simple blood test in order to check your thyroid. You may need medication from your family doctor.

Going through dramatic mood shifts. It is normal to experience mood swings throughout early motherhood. However, if you feel intoxicated or manic one minute, then angry or severely depressed the next with sharp distinctions between the two, get outside support.

Experiencing uncontrollable crying. If you are crying uncontrollably every day or every other day, or on the verge of tears frequently, dreading the dawn, dreading dealing with a wailing infant, you may have PPD. If you feel this fragile and nothing—rest, conversations with friends, loving touches from your mate—brings any relief, reach out to individuals who can help you overcome PPD.

Suffering anxiety or panic attacks. If you are experiencing panic attacks, immobilizing fear and anxiety, and sleeplessness because you have the feeling something bad is going to happen, contact someone as soon as possible. Make sure it is a person who is skilled with handling severe anxiety or a friend who is not frightened by intense emotions.

Experiencing severe separation anxiety. If you are terrified to leave your infant with another person, sure that harm will come to him, sure that you're the only person who can care for him, get some outside assistance. Fear this intense can inhibit your judgment and make you feel paranoid about leaving your infant to take care of yourself.

Obsessing about weight. If you are feeling angry about weight gain and find yourself cursing your body frequently, dieting strictly, or purging and bingeing, seek out help right away.

Fearing you are crazy. If you are having trouble holding a basic conversation, if you wonder whether others can tell that you're going crazy, if you fear those around you can see how deranged you feel inside and you feel like screaming for help, call a hot line immediately.

Enacting compulsive or obsessive behaviors. If you feel like you can't relax—constantly cleaning the house, talking on the phone, washing your hair, wiping down the counters, changing clothes, or doing anything to avoid feeling internal anxiety or to shut off continual negative mind chatter—call for help.

A Final Note to New Mothers

Remember: Postpartum depression is most likely to occur during the first two weeks following the birth of your baby, in the first two weeks before your period begins, and in the first two weeks after you have weaned your child. Be mindful of the onset of warning signals, particularly during these vulnerable times.

Resources:

Organizations
Depression After Delivery (DAD)
Nancy Berchtold, Founder
P.O. Box 1282
Morrisville, PA 19067
(800) 944-4773

Postpartum Assistance for Mothers (PAM)
PAM East Bay
P.O. Box 20513
Castro Valley, CA 95633
(510) 727-4610

PAM South Bay
15100 Lynn Avenue
Los Gatos, CA 95032
(408) 356-7872
(415) 948-8053

Postpartum Support International
Jane Honkiman, Founder
927 North Kellogg Avenue
Santa Barbara, CA 93111
(805) 967-7636

Clinics and Treatment Centers Specializing in PPD *in the United States*
Cass House Women's Center
133 Quaker Path Road
East Setauket, NY 11733
(516) 689-5664

Center for Postpartum Depression
33 Witherspoon Street
Princeton, NJ 08540
(609) 497-1144

Center for Postpartum Depression
2400 Chestnut Street
Suite 2203
Philadelphia, PA 19103
(215) 561-6381

Postpartum Moods Disorder Clinic
6635 Crawford Street
San Diego, CA 92129
(619) 287-2442

Clinics and Treatment Centers Specializing in PPD *in Canada*
Aid for New Mothers
P.O. Box 7282
Oakville, Ontario Canada L6J 6C6
(905) 897-6262

Calgary Postpartum Support Society
310-707 Tenth Avenue, SW
Calgary, Alberta Canada T2R 0B3
(403) 266-3083

Pacific Postpartum Support Society
Suite 104
1416 Commercial Drive
Vancouver, British Columbia Canada v5L 3x9
(604) 255-7999

Books

Ciaramitaro, Barbara. *Help for Depressed Mothers.* Edmonds, WA: Charles Franklin Press, 1982.

Dix, Carol. *The New Mother Syndrome.* Garden City, NY: Doubleday & Company, Inc., 1985.

Saavedra, Beth Wilson. *Meditations for New Mothers.* New York: Workman, 1992.

Scarf, Maggie. *Unfinished Business: Pressure Points in the Lives of Women.* New York: Ballantine Books, 1980.

Placksin, Sally. *Mothering the New Mother.* New York: Newmarket Press, 1994.

Magazine Articles

Leathe, Martha. "Postpartum Depression." *Mothering Magazine,* Spring 1987, 72-77.

Creating Total Health

Pregnancy is filled with moments when we look at our body and feel amazed that we can accommodate a growing person inside of us. We commend ourselves for the feats our body is performing in the name of motherhood. At other times, we look at our bulbous tummy and groan, feeling as if our body has been taken over. Especially toward the end of our term, we may experience backaches and neck pain that add to the discomfort of our enlarged abdomen. And we wonder how, after being so dramatically altered, our body will ever "find its way back." What we may not realize at the time is that we can assist our body throughout our entire pregnancy in ways that will make it easier for us to return to normal once our baby is born. Then, after our child's birth, there are many helpful options available to assist us in recovery and to help us achieve and sustain maximum health and well-being.

In this section, I cover a variety of holistically oriented modalities:

1. Chiropractic Care
2. Naturopathy
3. Massage Therapy
4. Homeopathy

These are professional services that are not generally provided by obstetricians, birthing classes, or midwives. I encourage you to explore the ways in which these specialties can greatly enhance the quality of your pregnancy, birth, and postpartum experience.

Chiropractic Care

Most of us, if we are familiar with chiropractic care at all, usually associate it with maintaining good posture. Or, perhaps, we have heard of someone who has received chiropractic adjustments because of a sports injury or automobile accident. But, for pregnant and postpartum women, chiropractic care can provide many benefits.

Pregnancy creates many structural changes in our body. We gain weight; our hormones cause our ligaments to become more elastic; and our muscles work harder. As a result, our spine can easily become misaligned. Not only does this create pain in our back and neck as well as other parts of our body, but it inhibits proper nerve functioning. Considering the fact that our nervous system controls every cell in our body, it is not difficult to see why proper alignment is necessary for good health. For example, if our adrenal glands become fatigued due to overuse (a common problem for pregnant women and mothers), we might experience chronic fatigue even if we are getting enough sleep (although, chances are, we are not getting all the sleep we need, and thus the problem is exacerbated). In this condition, we are more susceptible to a wide variety of negative physiological and structural changes owing to the adrenal glands' important role in many of the body's vital functions. Left untreated, our body will attempt to compensate and adapt to the changes, sometimes resulting in a greater imbalance. As chiropractor Dr. James LoConte of Palo Alto, California, attests: "It is very common for pregnant women to experience spinal problems, especially in their last trimester. Not only is there strain on their back and neck from the weight of the baby, but a hormone called 'relaxin' is loosening their ligaments so the baby may pass through the pelvis more easily. When ligaments are loose, there is more chance for misalignment; more subluxations occur. If any shifts in the body are not corrected, its structural integrity will be diminished, and the body's attempts to compensate for misalignment caused by pregnancy and childbirth can often create maladaptive problems that will persist into the future."

It is the chiropractor's job, then, to help maintain the structural integrity of a patient's body. For pregnant women and new mothers, this type of care is extremely beneficial. Not only does chiropractic care help to keep our structural alignment intact, thus avoiding unnecessary back and neck strain, but it helps to maximize the proper functioning of our nervous system—adrenal glands, hormones, and digestive functioning—at a time when we need them the most. When our internal systems are functioning properly, we will have a more rapid recovery from childbirth and be better prepared, physiologically, to handle the demands of caring for our children.

Health Advantages of Chiropractic Care

1. Alleviates back and neck pain caused by the weight of carrying a baby in utero as well as the strain of carrying and nursing an infant.
2. Assists in keeping the adrenal glands balanced when greater energy demands are placed on the adrenal system.
3. Alleviates strain on the joints, including lessening or eradicating the stiffness and soreness that are often the result of this strain.

4. Assists in maintaining hormonal balance during pregnancy and, more important, during the post-partum months. Chiropractic care is very effective when treating postpartum depression (PPD).

5. Counters the stressful effects of birth on the bones, joints, and muscles.

6. Corrects the condition that is a frequent result of cesarean sections. Because most cesarean sections require a great deal of pulling and tugging on the mother, her ribs, spinal vertebrae, and neck usually go out of place. Chiropractic adjustments can remedy this situation.

7. Helps correct misalignments and provides nutritional supplements when needed. Sleep deprivation can deplete the body of nutrients, including essential B vitamins that combat stress. This, in turn, can create misalignments within the body. A chiropractor can realign the body and can provide nutritional supplements to replenish the body as necessary.

How Do You Go About Finding a Chiropractor?

As with most professions, chiropractors offer a variety of styles and methods. Ultimately, you will have to decide what best suits your needs. However, I strongly recommend those chiropractic practitioners who utilize a method known as Applied Kinesiology (AK) or "muscle testing." The AK chiropractor offers the advantages of being well-trained in the traditional structural approach (giving adjustments), and also being able to assist you with matters of nutritional and emotional well-being. Those chiropractors who utilize Applied Kinesiology tend to take a more holistic approach and are skilled in dealing with a variety of physiological and emotional maladies common to pregnant and postpartum women. AK chiropractors also employ the methods of acupressure, utilizing the same pressure points as an acupuncturist does in order to stimulate organ, nerve, and energy centers within the body. But AK chiropractors do so without the use of needles. In addition, chiropractic care is covered by most medical insurance companies.

Naturopathy

Naturopathy is one of the most comprehensive holistic approaches to health care. Combining diet, exercise, herbal therapies, as well as a range of modalities designed to enhance emotional and psychological well-being, naturopathy contends that, given the proper environment, the body can heal itself and maintain optimum health. In short, a naturopathic physician takes a patient's entire lifestyle into account when prescribing treatment. The result is a specialized program for wellness based specifically on an individual's needs. Dr. Todd Nelson of Boulder, Colorado, offers this insight: "The main question a naturopathic physician asks is, 'How can I work with my patient to create a life that is most conducive to health?' And, together, my patient and I design a program to enhance the innate intelligence of the body. Not only does my patient's physical health improve, but she is given the opportunity to make changes that can create a more fulfilling and satisfying life." Because naturopaths tailor their health programs to the unique variables of each individual, it is common for them to ask for an abundance of information such as family history, lifestyle choices (including whether a person is fulfilled by work and personal relationships), and the amount of stress present in a patient's life.

Owing to the comprehensive nature of their work, naturopaths receive rigorous training in many areas of health: clinical nutrition, herbal medicine, homeopathy, acupuncture and acupressure, hydrotherapy, physical medicine (including therapeutic massage), counseling, lifestyle modification, and minor surgery. Obviously, this approach has many advantges. First, a naturopath can draw on this extensive training to construct a health plan that can adequately address a patient's wide-ranging needs. Then, the naturopath can actually implement many of the necessary treatments required. If outside help is indicated—perhaps chiropractic care or more traditional medical intervention—then the naturopath can recommend treatment in these fields to augment the patient's overall health plan.

Benefits of Naturopathy for Pregnancy

How can naturopathy benefit a woman during pregnancy? First of all, a healthy diet is essential during pregnancy. Expectant mothers require more nutrients to sustain their health and well-being. As Dr. Nelson points out, however, "The dietary information contained in many pregnancy books can be conflicting, thus making it difficult for the mother-to-be to determine what specific diet would most benefit her and her developing baby."

Naturopaths are nutritional experts who can devise a diet plan best suited to a pregnant woman's special needs. Should her needs change or special circumstances arise—anemia, for example—a naturopath can modify the woman's diet and provide emotional support through nutritional coaching. A naturopath can also determine whether a woman is properly assimilating her food and vitamin supplements. If a mother-to-be is taking the recommended vitamins, yet she cannot properly assimilate them owing to improper digestive functioning, toxicity in the bowel, or the wrong combination of foods, a naturopath can assist in eliminating these problems and improving the absorption of vitamins by both the expectant mother and her baby.

Another benefit to having a naturopath on an expectant mother's team is that a naturopath can decrease the frequency and severity of nausea and prevent the extreme fatigue pregnant women often experience through the use of nutritional supplements, herbs, homeopathy, and modified food combinations. If, for example, a mother-to-be is experiencing morning sickness, one simple change—eating proteins for breakfast instead of later in the day—could significantly reduce, or even eliminate, this problem. Also eating foods that are lighter, more easily digested, and combined well with other foods can give an expectant mother the nutrition she needs without empty calories. In this way, her energy is not tied up with digestion and can be utilized for other, more important things such as creating a healthy child, running a household, meeting deadlines at work, or enjoying her pregnancy.

Naturopaths are also trained extensively in counseling. A large part of their job is listening to their patients in order to identify prevalent psychological issues and to provide emotional support. By identifying which issues are creating stress in their patients' lives, naturopaths are better able to assist in alleviating psychological stress and helping patients come to terms with many personal issues. If a woman is experiencing anxiety about what kind of mother she will be because of her own family history, then a naturopath can offer short-term counseling to address this isssue. Should the woman require additional psychological support, the naturopath can direct her where to find that help. For women who come from dysfunctional families, this type of assistance can be invaluable because it is these women who are at greater risk for feeling conflicted about their mothering skills and more prone to postpartum depression. If these issues are confronted early on, then it is less likely a woman will be overwhelmed by them upon her baby's arrival. Again, preventive measures, the naturopath's forte, can make monumental life transitions go more smoothly.

Naturopathy and Postpartum

Today, many women are assembling a birthing team comprised of professionals from a variety of fields. Naturopaths can contribute a great deal to a woman's team. In some states naturopaths are licensed in prenatal and postnatal care. After your baby's birth, a naturopath can work with you to balance your hormones, naturally, using flaxseed oil, primrose oil, natural progesterone derived from wild yams, and other nutritional and herbal supplements. You will be less likely to experience the more frightening effects of emotional mood swings if your hormonal system is balanced. And, should you experience postpartum depression, you will have compassionate and knowledgeable support readily available to you. Here is a classic recipe used by naturopathic physicians to combat PPD:

Natural progesterone cream*
2 tablespoons flaxseed oil (borage oil or primrose oil) taken daily
Triaminosorb supplements (2 tablets two to three times a day)
Calcium, 1000 mg. per day
Magnesium, 500-600 mg. per day
Eat proteins in the early part of the day, lighter foods in the afternoon and evening.

Naturopaths can also provide valuable help if you are recovering from an emergency or routine cesarean section, assisting you in maintaining a healthy diet (despite the cafeteria food set before you) during your hospital stay in order to keep your immune system strong. This will make you less susceptible to infection and more resilient to the stress of early motherhood. Naturopaths can also address your particular needs as you begin to recover from birth, nurse your infant, and alter your lifestyle to make the transition into parenthood easier for both you and

*Progesterone cream often has dramatic results. However, it can be ordered only through a health-care practitioner and should be used under his or her guidance.

your partner. They know the importance of managing stress and self-nurturing. They know it is essential for a new mother to integrate her own care into her baby's schedule in order to keep herself strong and sane.

Massage Therapy

Massage therapy is one of the best ways to be nurtured by touch. The variety of styles (shiatsu, Swedish, deep tissue, or, among the more exotic, Ayurvedic Shirodaroa where warm oil is gently dripped on the forehead) have very different applications. Some methods focus primarily on physical and mental relaxation, while others are more directly therapeutic, focusing on specific muscles and chronic stress points. In other words, massage therapy can be used to throw away your cares and go into a deep state of relaxation or to correct specific problems such as aches and pains from sports injuries, stiffness and discomfort from everyday muscle strain, or tightness and restricted movement due to stress.

For pregnant women and mothers, massage is particularly helpful in alleviating soreness and restoring the vitality of the muscles by "getting the blood flowing." Even in the early stages of pregnancy, a growing baby can put stress on a mother's system. The initial fatigue we feel may cause us to slouch and hunch our back because our body wants to "get horizontal" instead of sitting at a desk, talking on a phone, attending meetings, or running to the grocery store. As a result, our body can become misaligned and certain muscles will try to compensate for this disequilibrium. After a time, the strain placed on these muscles can cause headaches, jaw tension, neck stiffness, pinching of the nerves, and other maladies that can intensify our feelings of lethargy. A massage can ease the muscles so they will return to a more relaxed state. In tandem with a chiropractic adjustment, many of the aforementioned symptoms will cease. And, because the chronic discomfort is gone, we will have more energy. In addition, rigorous massage can bring the blood to the surface and help our body eliminate toxins from our system through the skin—often these are toxins that can cause fatigue.

As pregnancy progresses, more strain will be placed on the lower back, knees, neck, and shoulders (especially if you gain as much weight as I did, going from 112 pounds to 172 pounds!). Muscles will need time to relax, not only by resting, but by being gently kneaded because it can be difficult for deep-muscle tissue to fully release tension on its own. In fact, some muscles can "lock" into a certain tautness, making it almost impossible to feel completely relaxed unless a therapeutic method such as massage, chiropractic care, or acupressure is applied. During the later part of pregnancy, deep relaxation is essential because the size of our belly makes it difficult to get a good night's sleep. Massage can help rejuvenate our mind and body even if we don't fall asleep. Why? Because it is *our* time to be touched and soothed. We do not have to reciprocate. There is no sexual pressure. (Some women prefer a female massage therapist for this reason.) And we do not need to talk or respond unless we are in the mood to do so.

In terms of labor and delivery, it is well-documented that a woman who is more relaxed during the birthing process is less likely to feel pain and discomfort. If you have been receiving regular massages throughout your pregnancy you will be able to reach a more relaxed state more quickly because you are "primed." This means that any tension that has been stored in your body can be released with massage so that when you are ready to give birth, less tension will have accumulated and you will be more apt to "let go" and relax into the contractions and delivery.

Where to Find a Massage Therapist

If you are currently seeing a chiropractor, you can ask your practitioner to recommend a massage therapist who would meet your needs. Many chiropractors have in-office massage therapists with whom they work in tandem. Naturopaths are also trained in massage therapy. Some specialize in various applications and can easily help you explore the methods of massage that would benefit you most.

Another option is to look for massage schools in your area. The teachers are usually very skilled, and you may have more styles of massage to choose from. If you have a local newspaper that runs advertisements for alternative health professionals, look for body workers who specialize in prenatal and postnatal massage.

Once you find a massage therapist you feel comfortable with, enjoy! Massage therapy can be one of the best tools for relaxation you will ever have simply because it feels good, and it helps both your body *and* mind slow down to a more soothing tempo of life.

Homeopathy

Homeopathy is a holistic system of medicine that was introduced in the late 1700s in Germany. Dr. Samuel Hahnemann experimented extensively with a variety of natural substances taken from plants, minerals, and animals, and his findings serve as the basis of homeopathy today. He discovered the "law of similars," namely that "like cures like." For instance, in its crude, undiluted form, arsenic is an acid that can create a burning of the tissues. In its refined, homeopathic form, however, arsenicum actually cures the very symptoms it brings on in its crude form—burning of the throat or burning sensation of the skin, for example. If a person is suffering from any type of a burning condition (burning of the nasal passages, throat, eyes, etc.) arsenicum is often the remedy indicated. Not only will it alleviate the burning symptoms, but, like all homeopathic remedies, it acts to stimulate the body's natural healing response, thereby creating greater overall health.

Interestingly, the more diluted a remedy is, the more potent it is. In the most potent remedies, the original raw material cannot be found, yet the remedy continues to be effective in treating illness.

Advantages of Homeopathy

As Christine Ciavarella, Certified Physician's Assistant, of Albany, California, says, "Homeopathy treats the person, *not* the illness." In other words, a homeopathic physician not only takes a patient's physical symptoms into account, but also emotional factors, lifestyle, particular stresses, phobias, and any other pertinent information that pieces together a holistic picture of the individual. Ms. Ciavarella adds, "Considering the holistic state of the individual allows a doctor to look at another human being in his or her entirety. That way, all the various components of the individual are taken into account in order to find common denominators that exist in disease. When a remedy is chosen, it will assist the individual on all levels, not simply the physical manifestations, or symptoms, that originally brought him or her into the office." The result is a gentle, non-toxic method of addressing physical maladies, emotional states, and overall health simultaneously.

Another benefit to homeopathic medicine is that many health-care professionals in this field have extensive conventional medical training. Some doctors of homeopathy are also M.D.s, thus offering "the best of both worlds."

Benefits for Pregnant Women

Homeopathy has many benefits for pregnant women. First of all, homeopathic remedies can treat problems such as bladder infections, viral infections, sinus infections, fevers, colds, flus, and other common ailments. Because these remedies do not contain any toxic chemicals, they do not pose a threat to a fetus like some pharmaceutical drugs do. According to *Alternative Medicine: The Definitive Guide*, "It is particularly effective in treating chronic illnesses that fail to respond to conventional treatment and is also a superb method of self-care for minor conditions such as the common cold and flu." Therefore, a mother-to-be can rely on homeopathic remedies for treating many common health problems without worry of injury to her child. In cases of prolonged exposure to viruses that cannot be erradicated by antibiotics or other conventional medicines, homeopathy can cure the problem long before the virus would be able to infect the fetus.

For expectant mothers who have problems with allergies, homeopathy can provide a welcome alternative to antihistamines and other potentially harmful drugs. Typically, a physician will recommend that a pregnant woman refrain from taking prescription drugs for the treatment of allergies until after her baby is born or, if she chooses to breast-feed, until after she has weaned her child. This means that she must tolerate chronic allergy symptoms such as sneezing, runny nose, congestion, watery eyes, fatigue, and throat irritation during her pregnancy, or risk introducing toxic substances to her baby. With the use of homeopathic remedies, allergy symptoms can be abated without ingesting harsh chemicals that have the potential of affecting the pregnancy.

Another advantage to homeopathic remedies is their ability to treat an individual's entire constitution rather than an individual's specific symptoms. A constitutional remedy acts to increase the quality of one's overall health and well-being. And when a mother-to-be's vitality is increased, the fetus's vitality will be strengthened.

An additional benefit of homeopathy is that it can treat physical symptoms and emotional states simultaneously. If an expectant mother is feeling anxious, restless, or fearful, there are specific remedies that can help soothe and balance her emotional condition. Should her emotions be causing physical symptoms such as stomachaches, headaches, hormonal changes, rashes, or acne, to name a few, a remedy can be prescribed that would both calm her and alleviate the symptoms.

Benefits for Birth

Homeopathy is commonly used by naturopaths, midwives, and birthing coaches during labor and delivery. In some cases homeopaths assist midwives and obstetricians during the birthing process with specialized remedy kits designed for helping the mother. There are remedies to assist the mother if her labor fails to progress, giving her an alternative to pitocin. Massage using acupressure points can also be used in conjunction with homeopathy to help labor progress. Some remedies help keep the mother's strength up during a long labor, while others alleviate fear and anxiety, which can cause unnecessary pain and discomfort during the birth. No matter how many remedies are used during childbirth, they will not hurt the baby. On the contrary, they can actually *help* the baby.

Applications of Homeopathy After Birth

Again, homeopathy has a variety of applications—all excluding the use of drugs. Remedies are effective when dealing with postpartum depression (not only for treatment of the emotional condition, but also for any physical symptoms that may arise due to tension, fear, and stress), breast infections, vaginal or anal discomfort, digestive problems, and many other maladies common to postpartum mothers. One remedy, known as "Rescue Remedy" (a flower essence used to calm and soothe), can be taken orally in those moments of crisis when a mother needs to restore her sanity. To this day, I keep a bottle handy!

Homeopathy is also safe for children and is often more effective than pharmaceutical drugs. This can make life easier for both mother and child. For instance, teething can create a great deal of pain for babies. Often mothers must deal with frequent tears, an irritable disposition, and fussy behavior which can be wearing. Chamomilla, a common remedy, often brings relief within minutes. Baby feels better, so mom feels better, too.

Another malady that responds very well to homeopathic treatment is ear infection, especially if ear infections have become chronic. (Also, in this instance, a few dietary changes can prevent future bouts with ear infections. You might want to consult a naturopath who specializes in homeopathy.) Croup, fevers, colds, rashes, and other common childhood illnesses are highly treatable homeopathically. Homeopathy can be a viable health-care alternative for you and your child.

Resources:

Chiropractic Care
American Chiropractic Association
1701 Clarendon Boulevard
Arlington, VA 22209
(703) 276-8800

California Chiropractic Association
7801 Folsom Boulevard
Suite 375
Sacramento, CA 95826
(916) 387-0177

The International College of Applied Kinesiology has a complete directory of chiropractors who employ the AK method in the United States and overseas. Contact:
International College of Applied Kinesiology
P.O. Box 905
Lawrence, KS 66044-0905
(913) 542-1801
(913) 542-1746 fax

Naturopathy
American Association of Naturopathic Physicians
2366 Eastlake Avenue
Suite 322
Seattle, WA 98102
(206) 323-7610

Institute for Naturopathic Medicine
66½ North State Street
Concord, NH 03301-4330
(603) 225-8844

National College of Naturopathic Medicine
11231 SE Market Street
Portland, OR 97216
(503) 255-4860

Massage Therapy
American Massage Therapy Association
820 Davis Street
Suite 100
Evanston, IL 60201-4444
(847) 864-0123

Homeopathy
International Foundation for Homeopathy
2366 Eastlake Avenue
Suite 301
Seattle, WA 98102
(206) 324-8230

National Center for Homeopathy
801 North Fairfax, Suite 306
Alexandria, VA 22314
(703) 548-7790

Books

Burton Goldberg Group, compiler; James Strohecker, Executive Director. *Alternative Medicine: The Definitive Guide.* Puyallup, WA: Future Medicine Publishing, Inc., 1994.

Cummings, Stephen, and Dana Ullman. *Everybody's Guide to Homeopathic Medicines.* Los Angeles: Jeremy P. Tarcher, Inc., 1991.

Kemper, Kathi J., M.D. *The Holistic Pediatrician: A Parent's Guide to Safe and Effective Therapies for the 25 Most Common Childhood Ailments.* Scranton, PA: HarperCollins, 1996.

Knaster, Mirka. *Discovering the Body's Wisdom.* New York: Bantam Books, 1996.

Lockie, Andrew. *The Family Guide to Homeopathy: Symptoms and Natural Solutions.* New York: Prentice Hall Press, 1993.

Northrup, Christiane, M.D. *Women's Bodies, Women's Wisdom: Creating Physical and Emotional Health and Healing.* New York: Bantam Books, 1994.

Ullman, Dana. *Discovering Homeopathy: Your Introduction to the Science and Art of Homeopathic Medicine.* Berkeley, CA: North Atlantic Books, 1991.

Ullman, Robert, and Judyth Reichenberg Ullman. *Patient's Guide to Homeopathic Medicine.* Edmonds, WA: Picnic Point Press, 1995.

Nurturing Touch

Remember back in high school when you took your first psychology class? One of the first things you learned about was the need for touch. To drive the point home, you were shown pictures of baby monkeys who had been removed from their mothers. Rather than eat or drink, these lonely little creatures preferred clinging to poorly constructed dolls made of scraps of fabric with button eyes. The sadness in these monkeys' faces was palpable. And you wondered why such a seemingly obvious fact—that touch is vitally important to humans and mammals alike—had to be proved scientifically. Your own subjective findings had born out the same facts. Touch feels great. You need it.

Nurturing, caring, loving touch, as the studies concluded, is an essential part of life for all sentient beings. Why, then, don't most of us get enough of it? Probably because we are too busy, or, we think we are too busy. Perhaps we think we can do without it. Or we may not think we need it. As one mother confided, "I just don't really think of touch as high on my priority list." However, as Denny Johnson points out in his book, *Touch Starvation in America*, "Touch is more than the physical sense of reaching with your hand and coming into contact with an object or person. Touch is also communication. Touch is association." Just as children can actually die from the lack of touch or an insufficient amount of touch, a part of us can shrink or wither if we don't receive touch. Adults need touch. Adults need to make contact. Physical touch as well as "connecting" through visual contact, tender and generous smiles, and verbal communication that "touches" the heart are all essential to our well-being. These methods of touching relax us; they rejuvenate us; they bring us pleasure; they let us know we are loved; they give us room to express who we are in a safe and nurturing environment. In addition, when we receive touch, when we feel touched, we can then extend these good feelings to others.

Mothers and Touch

Touch means different things to different mothers. New mothers often feel saturated by touch simply because they are in constant contact with their babies during the first six to twelve months of their newborns' lives. The sudden impingement on their free time can cause them to crave solitude, instead of interaction with others. Many new mothers, however, find that they also want the company of adults in order to stimulate their intellectual and conversational needs, especially during the first months of early motherhood. As one mother expressed it, "I need hugs and attention and good listening ears, just like my baby does. I need to know that others are aware of my needs, that they can anticipate them, and are able to fulfill them in a loving way." In other words, they need to be "touched" or attended to in ways that are nourishing to them, particularly at a time when they are giving out so much on a daily basis.

Speaking with mothers whose children were older, I heard echoes of the same sentiments. Certainly, for most of these women, the desire for love-making had increased, and this was one area in which they received touch. However, the variety of touch they needed, touch that was more reciprocal and less one-way, touch that was more mutually satisfying and nurturing, had increased. As one mother described it: "Becoming a mother made me more aware of my own needs for love and tenderness. As I became more aware of the many ways in which I touch others' lives—everything from hugs of reassurance to listening to my husband talk about work—I began to realize how multifaceted my own needs are."

What Touches You?

Take a few minutes to think about what touches you. Flowers? A movie that resonates with who you are? A call from a friend? A gift from your partner that is very personal? Feeling heard? Knowing that your children value you through certain demonstrations of love and gratitude? Watching your children show affection to their friends and their father?

Begin to pay attention to the things in your daily routine that touch you: a movie-star kiss from your child, a song on the radio, an enthusiastic response from your child's teacher for a project idea, whatever. Be sure to take these moments in. If you do not allow them to quickly pass without notice, their effect will linger with you throughout your day. As one mother of four put it, "It's the little things, the simple things that often keep me going."

Touching Oneself

Certainly, when we pay attention to all the small gifts sent our way in any one day, we feel grateful to be alive. The difficult moments don't seem insurmountable, we don't wish we were someone else, living someone else's life. We can take things in stride. Yet, there are those dry spells when we need to take the initiative and touch ourselves. For some, this may mean self-pleasuring: taking time to stroke your body and caress your face. You might even decide to bring yourself to orgasm with the loving stimulation of your own hands. If this idea feels foreign to you or brings up more anxiety than a sense of self-love, you might try this exercise.

Exercise

Make sure the house is empty to ensure that there will be no distractions or interruptions. (You'll also feel safer knowing no one will intrude and you won't have to deal with feelings of "getting caught" or having to explain what you're doing.) Remove your clothes and lie on the bed or on a soft blanket placed on the carpeted floor. If you feel more comfortable, put on a loose, soft sweatshirt, or wear a robe that opens in the front. Close your eyes so you can introduce yourself to your body through your fingertips and eliminate any unwanted distractions. (Some mothers told me they place family photos facedown in order to have more privacy.) Make sure the room temperature is warm enough for you to feel relaxed and uninhibited. If you want to create a more soothing atmosphere, light some candles or scent the room with aroma-therapy oils: chamomile, orange blossom, or lavender.

Envision yourself being completely taken care of as though you're in a womb-like environment, whatever that means to you. Perhaps you're lying in a grassy field full of colorful flowers, standing by a turquoise pool of water in a desert canyon, or rocking on gentle waves in a sailboat. In your fantasy, you need not be alone. Your lover can hold you, cradle your breast, tenderly lick your lips and caress your thighs. Instruct him if need be, tell him, silently or with your voice, what pleases you. Receive the gift of his touch throughout your entire body. Let him give to you.

When you feel relaxed and ready, begin to touch yourself on your face, then your neck and ears. Make circles with your fingertips on the balls of your shoulders. Cradle the roundness of your breasts; stroke your nipples; brush your hand along your belly and the sides of your waist. One by one, allow your fingers to glide over your hips and down your thighs. As you feel ready, move your hand between your legs and lovingly explore the beauty of your folds, and the wet opening of your vagina. Make love to yourself. Be your best lover. Receive the warmth and erotic pleasure that is your birthright. In the words of Louise Thornton, ". . . this is a gift. Life has given me this capacity for intense pleasure. I do not have to earn it or be ashamed of it or deny it. I am blessed and whole."

‎ꝛꝛꝛ

Resources:

Dodson, Betty. *Sex For One*. New York: Crown Books, 1996.

Johnson, Denny. *Touch Starvation in America: A Call to Arms*. Santa Barbara, CA: Rayid Publications, 1985.*

Thornton, Louise, Jan Sturtevant, and Amber Coverdale Sumrall, eds. *Touching Fire: Erotic Writings by Women*. New York: Carroll & Graf Publishers, Inc., 1989.

*To order Johnson's book write to: Rayid Publications, P.O. Box 1839, Goleta, CA 93116.

Helping Your Body Find
Its Way Back

Ⅰn the chapter "Creating Total Health," I discuss the benefits of chiropractic care, naturopathy, homeopathy, and massage therapy. If you haven't already taken advantage of some of the wonderful health-care options covered in that chapter—especially as they relate to pregnancy and postpartum care—you may want to read it. I am confidant that these forms of alternative medicine can offer you ways to increase your energy, to relax, and to improve your health and well-being. Take advantage of what alternative and complementary medicine has to offer. As the saying goes, "When Mom's happy, everybody's happy!" You can't lose. If you haven't already discovered the benefits of alternative and complementary medicine, I strongly urge you to explore this burgeoning field. Its applications for pregnant women and mothers are extremely helpful and can provide a nurturing element to health care which is often missing in more conventional modes.

In this chapter I will guide you as you begin the process of reclaiming your body and your own identity—your new identity as a mother. Part of claiming who you are as a mother is taking care of the needs you have, as a mother, and honoring this passage to its fullest.

Personal Identity

The bonding process between a mother and infant is an intense and consuming experience where, at least temporarily, our personal boundaries blur and our personhood bleeds together with our child's, like a watercolor painting. For a time, our life, our body, and our days are taken up by a little person who depends almost solely on us to meet all of his needs. It is no wonder we often have this nebulous feeling of "Who am I?" Yet, an individual sense of self emerges eventually, and we begin to take steps toward claiming our personal identities. For some of us, this happens when we finish breast-feeding, or when our baby is old enough to take food from someone else so that we can leave the house for several hours. Others find that after a certain period of time (and this varies for each individual), the initial chaos subsides and a routine is established. Still others describe the beginnings of the individuation process this way, "Suddenly, I began to notice that I could detect oncoming changes. I had entered a new phase of motherhood whereby I wasn't completely thrown for a loop whenever a new and unfamiliar situation arose. I suppose it was a certain confidence in myself . . . but it was more than that. I had actually come out of an all-consuming event, changed forever. I felt more like myself again." More often than not, our needs have changed, too. We are not exactly the same person we were before, but we're not completely different either. We have crossed a threshold in our development and are entering a new phrase of our lives.

Rites of Passage

Often some of our most significant life passages go unnoticed. We don't take time to honor their importance or reflect on the ways in which they have touched us and changed us. We don't take time to commend ourselves for coming into a new level of awareness, for learning and expanding. These inner passages rank low, if at all, on our priority list. Yet we wouldn't miss congratulating our children for learning to walk or talk, would we? Then why would we deprive ourselves of honoring our own accomplishments?

Reclaiming our bodies is an important part of reclaiming ourselves. It is a way to say, "I'm worth it. I matter." It is a way to respect being a mother as part of who we are and to embrace our own needs and individuality.

Ritual:
Reclaiming My Body

Purpose:
To Reacquaint Yourself with Your Body

Start by fully acknowledging your body, realizing that it is representative of many of the changes inside of you. You may want to remove your clothes if it's a warm day, and stand in front of the mirror. Perhaps this is the first time you've had to lovingly acquaint yourself with the many physical alterations that accompany pregnancy and childbirth. If you begin to criticize the bulk of your thighs and the girth of your belly, ask yourself, "Can I just enjoy the beauty today instead of ruminating about the need for an exercise program?" See if you can "lighten up" a bit.

I spoke with one mother who happens to be a model and actress (she knew how to "get into the part"); she would lift the creases above her cesarean-section scar and make them into a smiling face before the mirror. When she did this she experienced herself as "irresistible" in the same way she found her son's "apple cheeks" irresistible. Another mother, who claimed she could not draw, bought a piece of charcoal and, while looking in the mirror, moved the charcoal around the page in a way that she felt matched her curves and lines. The result was a beautiful self-portrait that she could come back to when she wanted to remember this particular passage. "I couldn't believe it! I actually captured myself on paper!" What about taking pictures of yourself in the nude? A young mother I spoke with had her best friend take black-and-white photographs of her in various poses. The pictures far exceeded either of their expectations—they were nothing short of beautiful. Then, they cut out the background and placed her figure on collages of other photographs—moonscapes with dolphins playing alongside her, flowers in bloom with her body at the center, fluffy clouds with her body floating as though it was weightless.

This is certainly a celebration ritual, and it need not be a solemn one. Try looking into your own eyes and drawing them in intimate detail: the flecks of color, dots of jewels, lines of flowers and fiber. What do they say about you? Looking into them do you see reflections of your soul? Do they tell you who you are now? Do they connect you with a visceral sense of what is stirring in you on the inside? Take some time to notice yourself; to thank yourself for going beyond your own comfort zone in order to rise to the duties, joys, and challenges inherent in being a mother. Be creative with this ritual. Use it as a way to bring yourself fully into this passage, like a compass that guides you home. Several mothers I was introduced to had made body casts of themselves (excluding their faces). One woman decorated her body sculpture with feathers, flowers, and beads; another woman painted a rendition of her own skin tones, nipple color, and tummy lines on the cast; and a third woman mounted her body on a stand, decorating the base of it with an elaborate design of stones, marbles, and shells.

If you can, take time to complete one of these projects, or perhaps a less daunting version of these projects, to mark the passage of this inner journey you have taken. As a mother, it is essential to always have a tangible reminder that while much of your time and devotion may go to others, you have an individual self who continues to grow and change and flourish—and this self needs to be admired and respected.

Assisting Your Body

The stress of motherhood is real. It can take an enormous toll on you physically, emotionally, and psychologically—not to mention the fact that it can test your faith and endurance. Yet, by being in touch with your body and its wisdom, you will learn how to better care for it. And when you know what your needs are, you can take the actions necessary to meet them. Your body is a bridge. There's a reason it is called "the temple of the soul." Whenever we do not take care of our physical health, our emotions are affected (and vice versa), we do not cope with stress as effectively, and our lives can become unmanageable.

During those times when you are "out of sync," go back to the photographs, drawings, or ways in which you touched your body or looked at it in the mirror (lovingly, without scrutiny), and let these recollections "bring you back" to an awareness of who you are.

Resources:

Northrup, Christiane, M.D. *Women's Bodies, Women's Wisdom: Creating Physical and Emotional Health and Healing.* New York: Bantam Books, 1994.

Dr. Northrup also writes a newsletter for women. For information, contact:
Women to Women
One Pleasant Street
Yarmouth, ME 04096
(207) 846-6163

Exercise

Exercise is an essential part of any mother's routine. Not only does it keep us physically fit by building our endurance and stamina, but it helps improve our outlook on life, giving us an "attitude adjustment" in a matter of minutes. Moving our muscles whether by walking, running, swimming, biking, dancing, roller-blading, or whatever your exercise of choice is, forces us to take in more oxygen which has a calming effect on our bodies and our brains. During exercise powerful endorphins are released throughout our entire system. As a result, we have more energy and are less likely to feel depressed and fatigued. Our vitality is increased, making us more resilient and better capable of handling whatever is thrown at us at work or home.

Breaking a Sweat

Rigorous exercise (not to be confused with overexertion) can be a mother's best ally because it clears the head and combats tension. Running or jogging can do wonders to rid the muscles of built-up stress and to alleviate constriction of the body's natural functioning. Even fifteen to twenty minutes two to three times a week can make a major difference in the way you feel.

Aerobic dance is also a healthy alternative if it is not too jarring. For many, low impact aerobics is preferable. Another advantage to aerobic dancing is that it can be done indoors, eliminating the weather factor, and it is enjoyable to have music help get you in the mood. Most health centers offer aerobic classes. Look for classes especially designed for new mothers. It's a great way to make new friends in your neighborhood—and no one will mind if your baby howls during the routines!

Swimming is also an excellent form of exercise because it utilizes nearly every muscle in the body, giving you a complete workout, and it has the least impact on your joints and muscles owing to the buoyancy of the water. In fact, injuries are rare for those who engage in this sport. Besides, the water, if not too heavily chlorinated, can have a soothing effect on your body as well as your mind.

If you like the water but are bored by lap swimming, you might try water aerobics. The resistance of the water builds your muscles while increasing aerobic activity, again with the least amount of stress to the body. Afterward, you can climb into the hot tub and relax for a few minutes.

Bicycling is another wonderful sport, and, unless you are traveling the backroads, the impact is low. You can also incorporate it into your daily routine. If you are with your child, you will both enjoy being outside instead of the usual car ride. Look for bike paths, especially if you live in an urban area, and explore a neighborhood you have never visited before. Or, what about running a few errands on your bike? You could strap saddlebags on the back to carry groceries, or you could place a bag or two in your child's riding seat.

Roller-blading is very popular right now, and it's no surprise why. It's fun. Who cares if you have to practice stopping by grabbing on to people you don't know or falling on the seat

of your pants? You can cover a lot of territory on roller
blades—and children enjoy them, too. When Alexander was
five years old, and his roller blades were several sizes too big,
he learned how to skate and could keep up with me. Together,
we put hundreds of miles on those skates. Just remember to
wear the proper gear: elbow and knee pads, helmets (especially
important for a child's safety), and wrist guards.

Walking

It's not unusual for mothers to complain of feeling "too tired
to exercise." Just the thought of putting on your swimsuit, driving to the pool, restyling your hair, and getting back to the
office can persuade you it is not worth the effort. During times
like these, consider walking (or hiking) as an alternative. The
benefits of walking should not be underestimated. You can walk
to the park with your children (even though they generally do
not walk in straight lines until they're at least four or five); you
can walk, pushing your child in a stroller; you can walk next
to your child as she rides her tricycle or bicycle; you can walk
the dog (believe me, they'll keep you exercising!); you can walk
to the local post office; you can walk during your lunch hour
while talking to a friend (feel free to complain about work or
plan your upcoming vacation); you can walk around the block.
A twenty-minute walk four to five times a week can keep you
in shape and calm your nerves just by getting you out in the
sunshine. Even a walk in the rain can be an invigorating experience. Put on your rubber boots along with your children and
jump in puddles. Let your hair get soaked.

   If hiking is more along your lines, put your small child in
a backpack and brave the trails. Or, let your children hike
alongside of you. They usually love the outdoors and it gives
them an opportunity to hunt for lizards, insects, frogs, deer,
hawks, and other wildlife. Besides, the sound of birdcalls rather
than honking horns can instantly relax you. You will feel

calmer, and as a result, your muscles will expand and you will take deeper and longer breaths. Don't forget, sunlight is a natural way to fight depression as it stimulates endocrine functions in the brain as well as in the glandular systems that control hormonal levels in the body.

Stuck Indoors

It happens to all of us: our child is ill and we have to care for him; the snow won't stop falling; or it's a holiday and the gym is closed *and* the clement weather predicted by the meteorologists is not materializing. Whatever the scenario, we're stuck indoors. Rather than give up on exercising for the day, consider these options:

Exercise with a video. The exercise video market has been flooded for the past five years, so a large selection is available. Consider Jane Fonda's low-impact aerobic workouts for expectant mothers (equally good for postnatal exercise). There are also exercise videos for children, and these can be fun for both of you. If you prefer stretching and strengthening routines, you might try Shirley MacLaine's video or the yoga exercise workouts made popular by Raquel Welch.

Use indoor exercising equipment. Nowadays you can purchase affordable, quality weight machines, step machines, and rowing machines. If you want to save up a bit, you could transform a room of your house into a respectable gymnasium. It's up to you. A run-in-place trampoline is also great (and kids love to jump on them), and they are less costly.

Do leg lifts and jumping jacks. Simple exercise routines continue to be effective because you can isolate muscle groups to strengthen and tone them. Try leg lifts for strengthening your abdominal muscles and your back (the combination is very helpful if you find yourself carrying your child on a regular basis). Lie down on the floor. Slowly raise your head off the floor by an inch or two. Then, with your knees slightly bent, lift your legs twelve inches off the ground. Hold them in the air for the count of ten, then slowly rest them on the floor. Do three sets of twelve to fifteen leg lifts, four to five times a week, and you'll notice a tremendous change. Jumping jacks are also an easy way to work your arms, legs, and lungs. They help to make your heart more efficient. Do them while looking out a window at the hummingbirds.

Do push-ups. Women groan at the mention of push-ups. I used to hate them, too. Then I discovered a wonderful way to do them in the bathroom where I won't be disturbed. The results are terrific! Here's how: Stand two to three feet away from your bathroom sink, depending on your height. Then place your hands on the edge of the sink and lean forward, supporting your weight on your arms. Find a position that is comfortable to you—no need to strain—and do push-ups off the sink. Work up to twenty-five to fifty push-ups three times a day. You'll be the one with the impressive biceps at the beach!

Do stomach vacuums. This exercise is great upon rising in the morning. It can help get you going by combining stretching, breathing, and using localized muscles. Stand with legs spread apart at a comfortable distance. Rest your arms at your side. Take a deep breath through your nose, filling your lungs and expanding your diaphragm. Hold for five seconds, then release the air through your mouth (slowly). Repeat three times. On the fourth breath, raise your arms straight above your head. Then, as you bend over, rest your palms on your thighs, slightly bend your knees, and suck in your stomach as tightly as you can while still holding your breath. Next, push your stomach out, draw it in, and balloon it out once more, then release the breath (you may need to take another, normal breath right away—go ahead). Do this three to five times a day. Not only will this rejuvenate you and clear your head, but it is a natural way to combat constipation—a typical symptom of stress.

Dance in the kitchen. If you want to raise your heart rate in an unstructured way, put on some dancing music and boogie through the house. Lifting my son up to be my dance partner built up my arms like you wouldn't believe!

Wrestle with your partner. I was raised on wrestling. It's famous in our family. It can give both you and your partner a workout—and it reduces tension. If you add tickling, it can make you laugh and forget the serious mood you may have brought home from work. If you can keep the intensity low, include the kids. Then everyone can have a good romp (if the weather is good and you are fortunate enough to have a lush lawn, wrestle outside in the fresh air).

No matter what exercise routine you choose remember, exercise is one of the best things you can do for yourself. It is not meant to be a punishment. It is meant to bring you back to your senses and bring you back into your body in a more relaxed way so you feel better. Don't worry about constantly meeting ideals ("I should be running five times a week," etc.), just enjoy yourself and have fun!

Resources:
Knaster, Mirka. *Discovering the Body's Wisdom*. New York: Bantam Books, 1996.
Lidell, Lucinda. *The Sensual Body*. New York: Simon & Schuster, 1982.

Balancing Your Body with Good Nutrition

One of the first things new mothers discover is how difficult it is to find time to eat, much less eat healthfully. Catering to a newborn, you often forget to eat, or you feel you don't have enough time to cook nutritious meals, so you scrimp on yourself. If you're not careful, these habits can persist until your own health is compromised or even diminished. Sound nutrition gives mothers the foundation they need to sustain the rapid pace of their life. Just as you monitor what goes in your child's mouth, be kind to yourself by being mindful of what you're feeding your body.

Protein. Mothers, especially if they are breast-feeding, need a sufficient amount of protein daily. Meat, eggs, fish, tofu, rice, and beans are good sources of protein. Candy bars, popcorn, and vanilla wafers are not. If you notice that you have a tendency to crave carbohydrates, especially foods full of sugar, whenever your energy is low, you may be "carbohydrate sensitive," meaning that although you desire starchy foods (pasta and potatoes) and sugary foods (cakes and cookies), what you probably need most is protein. Try it. Whenever you want to reach for a sweet snack, eat a hard-boiled egg, a chewy piece of turkey jerky (range-fed without additives), or tofu squares dipped in tamari sauce instead. You might also try a protein bar from your local health-food or specialty store. If you're watching your weight, you could fix a delicious smoothie made with cold vanilla soy milk and a heaping tablespoon of protein powder. If you prefer a fruit smoothie made with low-fat yogurt and protein powder*, consider these recipes:

Hawaiian Surfer Smoothie
1 ripe banana
2 medium slices of pineapple
2 tablespoons of papaya
1 cup fresh orange juice
1–1½ cups ice
½–¾ cup low-fat vanilla yogurt
2 tablespoons protein powder
Blend the first six ingredients together at high speed. Add the protein powder at the end.

Tropical-Blend Smoothie
¼–½ cup passion fruit juice
½ cup ice
¼ of a small pineapple, diced
½ cup low-fat vanilla or plain yogurt
1 tablespoon protein powder
First blend passion fruit juice and ice. Then add pineapple, yogurt, and protein powder.

---

*Spirulina, a blue-green micro-algae, is an excellent source of protein. It is also rich in folic acid and essential minerals and vitamins, including B_{12}. You can buy it at your local health-food store in capsule or granulated form. You might prefer to add it to your smoothie in place of protein powder.

❧ *Strawberry Paradise Smoothie*
5–7 large strawberries
¾ cup orange juice (or apple juice, if you prefer)
½ cup ice
½ cup strawberry kefir (liquid yogurt drink)
1–2 tablespoons protein powder
Blend the first four ingredients together and then add protein powder as you mix at high speed.

Mothers on the Run

It is not uncommon for mothers to get "quick energy fixes" from caffeine, sugar, and processed carbohydrates such as cookies, dessert cakes, and sweet breads. Unfortunately, these types of foods give you only a temporary energy boost, often leaving you feeling lethargic afterward. And, in order to push on, you reach for more of the same to propel you forward. Under these conditions, it is easy to develop a habit of eating unhealthful quick-energy foods to constantly keep yourself going. However, there are more nutritious alternatives.

Fruit. Fruit is an excellent alternative to sweets. Not only does it taste good, especially when fresh and in season, but the fiber content allows the fructose, or fruit sugar, to be released into your system gradually, thus avoiding the sharp highs and lows often associated with sugary foods and refined carbohydrates. If you're like me, you can easily tire of "an apple a day," so here are some other fruit suggestions:

❧ *Fruit Kebabs*
Take a wooden skewer stick and place a variety of cut fruit pieces on it to make fruit salad on a stick.

⅃⁎ Sort-of-Sorbet

Puree equal portions of strawberries and bananas (or, if you prefer blueberries and cantaloupe, pineapple and guava—whatever combination you desire) and place the mixture in small, individual portion bowls. Freeze. When you're hungry, enjoy the cold, fruity taste.

⅃⁎ Fruit Popsicles

1 cup strawberries
1 cup banana
2 cups low-fat vanilla yogurt or kefir

Puree one or two kinds of fruit. Add vanilla yogurt (or kefir) and stir. Freeze in popsicle makers. You may also want to cut small chunks of fruit to freeze in the yogurt or kefir base so you'll have pieces of fruit to chew while enjoying your popsicle.

Because fruit juices do not have any fiber to regulate the sugar levels entering your bloodstream, you may want to dilute them with bubbly mineral water. Pretend you're on a beach in Hawaii enjoying a froufrou drink. Paper umbrellas are optional.

Other healthful energy-booster drinks include peppermint tea (iced or hot), orange and lemon hibiscus tea, rosehip and lemon tea, and spearmint and orange tea. These drinks also contain vitamin C. If you wish to sweeten them, try apple juice, or a small amount of granulated fructose (fruit sugar).

Consider this: both sugar and caffeine overstimulate your adrenal glands, creating imbalances that can quickly lead to a burnout of these important glands. Since B vitamins are essential for the production of adrenaline, your body can quickly be depleted of the very vitamins that help you to reverse the effects of stress (B vitamins). If you are not already taking a B complex supplement, you might want to look into one that meets your particular needs.

If you tend to be a natural "grazer," eating small meals or snacking throughout the day, that could be the basis for a diet that prevents severe fluctuations of blood-sugar levels. You may want to plan to have six small meals throughout the day rather than three large ones. A "meal" could consist of a large apple; a cup of instant soup (try to find a brand without sucrose, dextrose, MSG, or other additives); an almond and raisin mixture; celery sticks with tahini sesame spread; a small portion of pasta and vegetables; tuna salad with fresh, raw veggies; scrambled eggs; or a breast of chicken with buttermilk sauce and carrot sticks; to name a few ideas. If you work outside your home, plan ahead and carry several mini meals with you so you're not tempted to subsist on coffee and donuts until you return home to a large meal before bed.

Healthful Snacks for Mothers on the Run

- Carrot sticks
- Celery with sesame tahini butter spread (high in calcium)
- Coconut or almond rice pudding (instant mixes from a health-food stores or made fresh)
- Almonds (high in calcium)
- Sunflower and pumpkin seeds (a good source of iron and calcium)
- Raw vegetables (cucumbers, squash, broccoli, carrots)
- Apple slices dipped in fruit yogurt or sesame butter
- Dried apricots, papaya, and apple slices
- Strips of baked chicken over olive oil and garlic pasta
- Protein bars
- Low-sugar cookies made with rice or multigrain flour
- Grapes (preferably organic)
- Organic greens with orange slices and almonds (mustard-honey, orange-honey, or soy-orange dressing)
- Pistachio nuts

- Fresh orange, pear, papaya, mango, honeydew melon, or banana (rich in potassium, vitamin C, and digestive enzymes)
- Rice cakes (flavored, or spread almond or sesame butter on a plain rice cake, then place apple slices on top)
- Chilled beets (great source of iron)
- Popcorn or chips that have not been fried
- Prunes (great source of iron and good for the intestines)
- Soy sausage (good source of quick protein and can be cooked in a microwave)

Healthy Meals

Obviously, nutritious meals are the foundation for health. If you go to any bookstore you will find vegetarian cookbooks, low-fat cookbooks, high-energy foods cookbooks—everything imaginable. Take some time to browse and find recipes that would suit you and your family. If your family is accustomed to macaroni and cheese, hot dogs and potato chips, and grilled cheese sandwiches with carrot sticks, don't suddenly put a rice, bean, and tofu medley in front of them and expect them to enthusiastically plunge in. Transitions take time. Slowly, alternate between the foods they have come to enjoy and more healthful versions of the same thing. For example, try soy cheese as a substitute for dairy cheese, especially if chronic colds, ear infections, and allergies are common among your brood. What about soy hot dogs or turkey hot dogs that do not contain monosodium glutamate? Potato chips that are baked, not fried? And pasta with a few thinly sliced vegetables in addition to that creamy cheese sauce?

Also, if you are serious about revamping your diet along with your family's, consider contacting a naturopathic physician in your area since they are nutritional experts. If you are already seeing a health-care practitioner such as a homeopath, chiropractor, or acupuncturist, ask for diet recommendations as well as herbs and supplements that could improve your health.

Vitamins and Supplements

I strongly recommend a comprehensive nutritional supplement for women, designed by a woman, called "Fem Multi." It is distributed by Metagenics and can only be purchased through a licensed health-care professional. Although it is specifically designed to reduce the negative effects of premenstrual syndrome (PMS), it also can serve as a daily supplement because it contains essential vitamins and minerals necessary for women's particular health needs.

You should also make sure these vitamins are included in your diet:

B vitamins. These are important for busy mothers to reduce stress.

Vitamins C, D, E, and A. These vitamins assist the body's immune system, help with healthy cell production, strengthen our teeth and bones, and prevent illness. Vitamin D is required for the absorption and utilization of calcium. Deficiencies can contribute to osteoporosis and deterioration of the joints.

Minerals are also important for maintaining optimum body functioning. Be sure to look for a supplement that contains these minerals:

Magnesium. This helps with nerve functioning, among other things.

Potassium. This helps to treat high blood pressure and maintain cellular integrity.

Selenium. This antioxidant mineral partners with vitamin E to help protect cell membranes; it also stimulates immune response.

Copper. This is necessary to the formation of blood cells and the maintenance of healthy skin and hair.

Zinc. According to James J. Gormley, zinc is "involved in over 200 of the body's enzymes; this mineral: helps maintain the health of our eyes, skin, hair and joints; stabilizes cell membranes against free-radical damage, thereby boosting our immunity; improves reproduction successes; reduces menopause-associated depression. . . ."

Iron. This is essential for healthy blood.

Many of the healthful snacks I have listed are rich sources of the vitamins and minerals essential for women's good health. Of course, there is a variety of fresh foods and recipes to enhance their taste that you might want to pursue—everything from collard greens (high in calcium and iron) to beans and legumes (complex carbohydrates and proteins).

Resources:

Cookbooks
Cooks, Natalie Dupree. *Quick Meals for Busy Days*. New York: Clarkson Potter, 1996.
Taylor, Mary. *New Vegetarian Classics: Entrees*. Freedom, CA: Crossing Press, 1995.
Waters, Alice. *Chez Panisse Vegetables*. New York: Harper-Collins, 1996.

Books
Feinstein, Alice, ed. *The Healthy Woman*. Emmaus, PA: Rodale Press, 1994.
Jacobson, Michael F., and Bruce Maxwell. *What Are We Feeding Our Kids?* New York: Workman Publishing, 1994.

Lieberman, Shari, and Nancy Bruning. *The Real Vitamin and Mineral Book: Going Beyond the RDA for Optimum Health.* New York: Avery Publishing Group, 1990.

Reuben, Carolyn, and Joan Priestly. *Essential Supplements for Women: What Every Woman Should Know About Vitamins, Minerals, Enzymes and Amino Acids.* New York: Perigree Books/Putnam, 1988.

Warner, Penny. *Healthy Treats and Super Snacks for Kids.* Chicago: Contemporary Books, 1994.

Spa Secrets

Let's face it, while all of us dream of spending days being pampered at a spa, few of us actually get the opportunity. It either costs too much or requires too much time away from our families and work. But, before you give up on luxuriating altogether, think about turning your own bathroom into a spa of sorts. It doesn't require extensive preparation, and once you have the essential ingredients, you'll be set to go.

Ingredients

Essential oils have an ancient history. For centuries they've been used to soothe and heal all types of ailments. They also have energizing properties and are a simple, yet effective pick-me-up. In the information that follows, I concentrate on a variety of bath-blend recipes. However, if you are in a rush, sprinkle several drops of your favorite essential oil on a washcloth or sponge and gently spread it over your body from head to toe. You may also want to buy a bottle of aromatherapy mist—orange blossom, rose water, or jasmine—to spray on your face, neck, breasts, and behind after finishing your shower. You can even apply mists at the office.

Your local health-food store should carry a wide selection of essential oils, sea and mineral salts, as well as unrefined organic "carrier oils" (cold processed oils that can be mixed with essential oils for massage and skin application). If you can't find what you need, contact the companies listed at the end of this chapter for mail orders.

Recipes for Relaxation

☙ *Calming Bath Blend*
4 drops chamomile oil
4 drops lavender oil
2 drops orange oil
1 drop tea tree oil

☙ *Workaholic Bath Blend*
2 drops lavender oil
1 drop neroli oil
1 drop geranium oil
1 drop clary sage oil

☙ *Invigorating Bath Blend*
3 drops rosemary oil
2 drops thyme oil
2 drops tea tree oil
1 drop peppermint oil or 2 drops lemon oil

☙ *Nervous Tension Bath Blend*
3 drops neroli oil
4 drops clary sage oil
4 drops ylang-ylang oil
2 drops chamomile oil

☙ *Perfumed Garden Bath Blend*
3 drops ylang-ylang oil

3 drops jasmine oil

3 drops neroli oil

✦ *Hormonal Balancing Bath Blend*

3 drops vetiver oil

2 drops geranium oil

2 drops sandalwood oil

✦ *Sensual Scented Bath Blend*

3 drops sandalwood oil

2 drops jasmine oil

2 drops lemon oil

Health and Beauty

The Hawaiians are well-known for their healing traditions. As my Grandma Mamo used to say, "Get in the ocean and she'll heal whatever ails ya'."

To cleanse your system by allowing the toxins in your body to be gently released through your skin, try the following bath soaks:

✦ *Hawaiian Cleansing Bath*

2 cups sea salt (Dead Sea salt is great, too)

2 cups epsom salt

½ cup seaweed powder

Add the scents you like best.

After soaking for twenty to thirty minutes, take a shower to wash off any impurities released from your body. You may wish to gently run a skin brush over your body to remove dead skin. This will revitalize your skin, making it softer and smoother.

✦ *Cellulite Reduction Bath Blend*

¼ cup seaweed powder

4 drops lemon oil
2 drops cypress oil
2 drops fennel oil
2 drops rosemary oil
Again, I would suggest that you take a shower after soaking, using a bath brush to stimulate your muscles and tissues, so the toxins (which cause cellulite) can be flushed out of your body. (Roberta Wilson includes this bath blend in *A Complete Guide to Understanding and Using Aromatherapy for Vibrant Health and Beauty.*)

✷ Honey-Almond Skin Scrub
1 tablespoon almond meal
1 tablespoon honey
1 drop lavender oil
Blend all of the ingredients together in your palm until a paste is formed. After cleansing your face, apply the skin scrub. Gently massage the mixture in for one to two minutes, then rinse thoroughly.

✷ Facial Toners
½ cup distilled water
3 drops frankincense
   or
½ cup distilled water
3 drops geranium oil
Add the essential oil to the distilled water in a sterile bottle. Shake. Dampen a cotton ball with mixture, then apply generously to your face. Both of these essential oils are known for their ability to heal and rejuvenate the skin.

While soaking in a hot bath, it feels wonderful to cool off your face with a washcloth.

You may also want to look to nature's own special facial foods (oatmeal and avocados):

✢ *Oatmeal Facial Mask*
2 cups oatmeal
5 drops almond oil
4 drops rosemary oil
Cook oatmeal (a slightly loose and squishy consistency is best). Allow the oatmeal to cool down to room temperature. Then chill in the fridge. When your bath is ready, remove oatmeal and add almond oil and rosemary oil and blend. Apply the mixture. Rinse after ten to fifteen minutes.

✢ *Avocado Facial Mask*
1 ripe avocado
3 drops jojoba oil
2 drops bergamot oil
Mix ingredients until smooth. Apply to the face for five to ten minutes. Rinse thoroughly.

Be sure to cleanse your face before applying these masks. I highly recommend "Foamy Herbal Cleanser" that can be ordered through Jamie Gordon Skin Care Studio in Boulder, Colorado: (303) 440-0969. Jamie specializes in pure and natural skin care products and offers a "Home Facial Kit."

Resources:

Books
Cox, Janice. *Natural Beauty at Home.* New York: Henry Holt and Company, 1995.
Fischer-Rizzi, Susanne. *Complete Aromatherapy Handbook: Essential Oils for Radiant Health.* New York: Sterling Publishing Co., Inc., 1990.

Wilson, Roberta. *A Complete Guide to Understanding and Using Aromatherapy for Vibrant Health and Beauty.* New York: Avery Publishing Group, 1995.

Mail-Order Companies

Ahava
2001 West Main Street
Stamford, CT 06902
(800) 252-4282
(203) 357-1914

Aroma Vera
5901 Rodeo Road
Los Angeles, CA 90016-4312
(800) 669-9514
(310) 280-0407

Arrowhead Mills
P.O. Box 2059
Hereford, TX 79045
(800) 858-4308
(806) 364-0730

Jamie Gordon Skin Care Studio
2727 Pine Street
Suite 7A
Boulder, CO 80302
(303) 440-0969

Sex and Intimacy

For mothers, learning how we want to be touched is of utmost importance because touch, in its many forms, can nurture and revitalize. It can heal us and bring us back to our center. It can allow us to give and receive in meaningful ways, especially during those times when we feel like all we do is dispense kindness and love to everyone but ourselves. Furthermore, touch is communication. It can create a bridge for closeness. It can open the gates to clearer, less defensive heart-to-heart talks. And, if we so desire, it can turn into intimate, joyful, and passionate lovemaking.

Cycles of Sex and Intimacy

We live in a culture that often forgets about the cycles of life and, instead, focuses on events and personal history as if they traveled a linear path. Yet, for most of us, our lives rarely move from point "A" to point "B." Rather, we take detours, incur surprises, and backtrack on our way to point "B," sometimes landing on point "C" with no idea how we missed our original destination. For this reason, it is helpful to learn what our needs are on different days as well as during different periods of our lives. This approach honors and respects the natural cycles that we, as women, experience. And, it helps us to avoid the unnecessary trap of feeling that we always need to be the same and respond in the same way regardless of the circumstances or time of the month.

As mothers, our needs for touch and intimacy are constantly changing. What feels good one day might not be the best approach later in the week. Our feelings change. Our level of fatigue increases and wanes. Some days are hectic while others have room for setting aside time for mutual enjoyment. Often, it is these variables that cause our needs and desires to fluctuate. Think about it. Even our ovulation cycle translates into different needs during different times of the month. Some of us have a peaked interest in playful and amorous lovemaking right before our period while others prefer solitude and alone time. Still others want to be close to their partners, yet, due to high levels of stress, or a more gentle mood, they want intimacy in a nonsexual way. In other words, they want to be lavished with kisses and caresses without any pressure to have intercourse. Some mothers long for hours of luxurious lovemaking with their partner, while busy mothers often feel indifferent about sex for a certain period of time. Knowing what one's cycles are and being clear about the need for touch, including the type of touch that is desired, is essential.

Howling at the Moon

That women have cycles is common knowledge. Jokes about PMS are peppered throughout sitcoms as are story lines that accentuate the absurd predicaments that can result from women's fickle mood swings. Sometimes we just have to take it all in stride and confess: "Yes, it's that time of the month. Excuse me while I howl at the moon!" What we don't need to do, however, is chastise ourselves for the different moods and needs we have during the course of our monthly cycle. Instead, when we adhere more closely to our bodies' needs, life flows more smoothly. For example, if we have bouts with PMS whereby we often cry and release anger, why don't we consider this a detoxifying mode for our mind and body rather than declaring ourselves "crabby old ladies"? Viewed in this way, we can make allowances for our behavior and take responsibility for finding ways to buffer its effect on others (taking a hot tub at the gym, going for a run, or doing some needlepoint) or explore avenues for safely expressing our feelings (talking with a close friend, problem-solving with a partner, or confiding in a therapist). In addition, we might try natural remedies for curbing the extreme behavior alterations so our lives will not be as intensely disrupted. This can be done with the help of chiropractic care, naturopathy, homeopathy, and massage therapy (or some combination of these and other alternative health-care modalities—see the chapter, "Creating Total Health"). I suggest trying the following exercise for a few months. It's simple, yet it can be very illuminating.

Exercise

Charting your monthly cycles. By now, the majority of us have wall calendars pinned up in strategic locations throughout the house. Find a calendar that has some space left in its little boxes (or buy one with larger daily slots), and jot down your mood for the day. It doesn't have to be a lengthy description. One or two words will do. For example: "cranky," "tired," "preoccupied by work," "longing for rest," "wanted to be held," "wish someone would stroke my hair," "energetic," "happy," "peaceful," "balanced," "wanted to play," "fantasized about having wild sex in the kitchen," "impatient," "no tolerance for screwballs," "wished I was single again," "slow boat to China sounds appealing," "life sucks," "restless," "need to break loose from my routine," "felt tender and loving," "spaced-out," etc. Then, after several months, see if you can detect any general pattern. Do you have more energy right before or after your period? Does your anger reach a crescendo during any particular phases of the month? Do you feel serene when you have your period? Or irritable? Is your body more sensitive on certain days? Do your sexual feelings peak at any particular time of the month? When is gentle touch more appealing than passionate advances? When do you resent demands? When do you feel capable of handling whatever comes your way? Think about these questions. Then take a few minutes to chart out general sections of the month where you are more prone to certain feelings and temperamental attitudes.

Next, if possible, make some alterations in next month's schedule. How about that big presentation at work? Could it be put on the calendar after your period if that is when you have more energy and are more likely to handle criticism with poise? Could your partner plan to take the children to the local fair at the onset of your menstrual cycle so you could sleep in and rest in bed? If exercise helps minimize your PMS symptoms, could you plan on taking a few extra walks around the neighborhood? Go to swim at the YMCA? Do some aerobic exercises in front of the television while your baby is busily gumming teething biscuits? It is highly likely that any accommodations you can make, even seemingly small ones, will make things run more smoothly for you and your family. You will also be better able to take advantage of the times when you and your partner can be close because, during certain times of the month, you will be more predisposed to relaxing and more likely to initiate physical and emotional intimacy.

ॐ ॐ ॐ

Another part of the equation is looking at where you are in terms of motherhood. Are you a new mother? Do you have two active toddlers? Is one child in school while the other one is cared for by a child-care provider or a relative for a portion of the day?

New Mothers

If you are a new mother, your needs are different than those mothers who have older children. First of all, you may be experiencing touch saturation. This can be especially intense for mothers who are breast-feeding. You may be in continual contact with your infant for prolonged hours during the day. The last thing you are interested in is more physical contact when the lights go out (especially if you know they won't stay out for any length of time). Also, vaginal dryness can be a problem. Owing to changing hormonal levels, vaginal lubrication is frequently reduced, making penetration uncomfortable, or, in some cases, painful. For this reason, it is important to let your partner know what you are experiencing as a result of childbirth and ask that he take these physical concerns into account. Lengthier touching and kissing and tender breast stimulation are ways to give your body more time to become moist if you and your partner want to include intercourse in your lovemaking. Of course, saliva works well and feels wonderful. And, if necessary, K-Y jelly and other lubricants can be helpful.

Lastly, exhaustion can definitely put a damper on amorous feelings. You may wish to be touched, but in a way that feels most giving to you. Take some time to let your partner know that, while you want to be close, you may not have as much energy as you would like at this particular phase of motherhood and that it would help you if he took a more active role in nurturing you. Reassuring your partner that you are not rejecting him, but rather that you are physically and emotionally exhausted, can let him know you wish to be intimate without any sexual pressure until you catch up on sleep.

Allowing time to heal. An essential part of restoring your ability to give and receive sexually is allowing yourself ample time to heal from childbirth. Granted, many women "bounce right back" a few weeks after delivery. Yet many of us need rest and recovery time, especially if we underwent extensive surgery. If lovemaking enhances your healing process, then by all means, enjoy, and make it an integral part of your recovery (I give suggestions for ways to do this later in the chapter). On the other hand, if sexual demands or persistent requests inhibit your full recovery, making you feel depleted from giving out too much to too many others too soon, then respect your limits and communicate them to your partner. Take steps to avoid having your healing process disrupted by discussing your experience with your partner. Let him know how much work is involved in caring for an infant, and continue to reassure him that you love him and desire him as a lover.

Setting limits. Men often express their need for closeness sexually. They want to be inside of us. It makes them feel safe and secure; it makes them feel loved and cared for. To men, physical and emotional needs can feel like one and the same thing. While some men have explored a wide range of ways for giving and receiving loving and erotic touch, many have not. And, if you are a new mother, chances are you are not up for teaching your partner other ways to be close—who has the time?! You might suggest that your partner read this chapter and look into learning some of the methods of getting one's emotional needs satisfied through a variety of intimate touch. But, if he persists in pressuring you or tries to make you feel guilty for not meeting his needs, this can wear you down and prolong the healing process indefinitely. In extreme instances where a partner doesn't respect a new mother's personal boundaries and blames her for not meeting his needs, using accusatory statements such as "All my friends say they had sex with their wives within the first two weeks of their baby's birth. It's not right that you want to wait," she may need outside support. Perhaps a brother or a father or a close male friend could provide the necessary words to help him become more patient and accepting of the changes in both of your lives and the ways in which these changes affect your relationship. Another approach might be discussing, in very concrete terms, why you may not be interested in sex or even feel capable of enjoying it at this time. For instance, let your partner know that if he prepared dinner and cleaned up afterward, giving you time to rest, you would have more energy for lovemaking. With talks such as these you can make it clear that if you are getting some of your basic needs met, such as sleep and good nutrition, you will be better able to give to your partner in other ways.

Feeling like a nun. Over the years I've noticed that many new mothers express a fear that they will never be the sexually active women they were before giving birth, not realizing how substantially their lives have been altered by the advent of motherhood. When I explain that it may take a little time before their interest in making love peaks, they still want more reassurance. "I used to straddle myself on my husband's lap while we drove on the highway at night," one woman told me, waiting for me to explain to her in tactful terms that those days were over. "We'd come home for lunch and do nothing but make love the entire time"—more proof that their sex life was always going to be dismal. After some of the not-so-new mothers gave their personal testimonies, these new mothers began to entertain the possibility that their worst fears might not be realized. In fact, the not-so-new mothers agreed that in many ways their sex lives had actually improved. At this, the new mothers shook their heads. "Inconceivable," they declared, deciding that the rest of us had been lying to them all along. Fortunately, years later, several of the new mothers I'm referring to here called to let me know that, much to their surprise and delight, those not-so-new mothers had been right. (Although they were quick to point out that not everything was *the same*. What could I say? I've gotten old enough to see, firsthand, that change is inevitable.)

Not-So-New Mothers

Eventually, as mothers pass through the postpartum months and become more experienced, they begin to see more of an ebb and flow to their lives, realizing that while difficult periods may persist, they rarely last forever. It becomes clear that while there are some things we can change, there are some things we cannot. Differentiating between the two can save mothers a great deal of frustration (and, thus, inner stress) and can open up more creative avenues for moving life in the directions we want it to go. As a mother of twins put it: "The picture will always be changing. Having a varied repertoire from which to draw on, especially when times are tough, is the key."

Exploring Options For Sensual and Loving Pleasure

Undeniably, our circumstances have changed. Children do that. But that doesn't mean we have to accept celibacy as a way of life. Nor do we have to pile sex on top of an already over-crowded schedule, resigning ourselves to "quickies." Instead, try thinking about the alterations in your lifestyle as opportunities to explore options for sensual and loving pleasure. You may discover that your lovemaking can be richer, more mutual, and more fulfilling as the quality of your communication improves and your relationship is strengthened.

Writer Margaret Atwood once said, "The Eskimos had fifty-two names for snow because it was important to them: there ought to be as many names for love." The same is true for lovemaking. We tend to limit its vast importance and diverse applications in our lives by conveniently placing it under the umbrella term of "sex," which primarily focuses on the genitals and intercourse. But making love means so much more.

And, believe it or not, becoming a mother is an opportune time to enhance your intimate life with your partner by making it more conscious and loving. To clearly communicate what your sexual and sensual needs are, and to become more comfortable with them, makes room for more spontaneity and, eventually, as you create spaces of time, more exploration.

Sensual Touch

Phyllis K. Davis, in her book *The Power of Touch,* has this to say: "My message for you can be summed up in three words: *touching is loving.*" Sensual touch is incredibly loving. It bathes your senses in magical, affectionate, and kind strokes given freely from the hand, yet deeply felt in the heart. It is not rushed, but savored, and can be brought to the levels of sacred reverence, if that is your intention.

I know for mothers and their partners it is sometimes difficult to imagine having the time and private space to luxuriously dwell in each other's company, taking each moment to fully focus on one another's body. Although it is not necessary to spend hours covering every inch of each other, you may want to, on occasion. One couple I've known for years have a baby-sitter or a relative take their two children out to dinner and a movie once a month (usually in the late afternoon) so they can have a "date" at home. This allows them intimate time together in familiar surroundings. Sometimes they read out loud to each other in bed in the nude. Other times they spend hours reacquainting themselves with their bodies through touch and slow, artful lovemaking. If they want to take a bubble bath and wash each other's bodies and then go out for a candlelit dinner, then they do that instead of spending the entire time in the house. Another couple I know likes to go hiking together first. Then, after exercising much of the pent-up stress out of their bodies, they lie naked, touching and kissing until they fall into each other's arms and go to sleep. They wake up feeling refreshed, close, and tender with each other. They've told me, "This sets the tone for the rest of our week."

Exercises

Arm tickles. Remember going to slumber parties with all your best girlfriends? Remember after the pizza and television and gossip and giggles died down nobody could sleep because of the excitement? Then someone would perk up and say to the group, "I know what we can do. Arm tickles!" Whereupon only the uninitiated didn't volunteer an overly enthusiastic shout of "Yes!" Well, arm tickles are still great, not only for friends, but for couples (and restless children) as well. First, turn your palm upward (or have your partner turn his palm upward if he is going first). Lie down or lean into a soft pile of pillows or even sit on a couch or chair where you can comfortably slouch. Then ask your partner to lightly caress your forearm with his fingertips (a feather can also be used). If it tickles too much, have your partner apply more pressure. Try to find a pressure of touch that both relaxes and gently stimulates. Experiment to see if you and your partner can find that fine line between tickling and erotically soothing each other. You know that look dogs have when you rub their stomachs? A cross between ecstasy and stupefied bliss? That feeling is your goal. (Who cares what your faces look like?!) You can move your hand up and down or from side to side, waving your fingers like sea anemones, or keep your fingers relatively stationary and simply move your hand up and down the forearm. This type of sensual touch can be applied to all areas of the body. If you discover areas that are initially too sensitive to such light touch, then spend a little time experimenting with different pressures. You may find that, eventually, those areas that "couldn't handle it" without feeling ticklish soon become your favorite places to be touched.

࿐࿐࿐

Cupping. One very tender and intimate form of sensual touch is "cupping." You can use your hands to "cup" or cradle each other's faces, breasts, testicles, buttocks, thighs, feet, hands, stomach, hips, etc. As you've probably already noticed, infants and children thoroughly enjoy cupping their mother's face and breasts because it makes them feel close and loved, and it is a way to express their loving feelings nonverbally. With this in mind, try the following exercise. First, fully clothed, sit across from each other in comfortable positions (use chairs or sit on the floor—whichever you prefer). Look into each other's eyes without saying a word. Initially, you may feel a bit awkward or self-conscious. You may laugh or find ways to distract yourself from the exercise. You or your partner may even feel somewhat guarded. These are all normal responses. It may take a few minutes to relax and let your defenses down. Shedding one's armor can take a little time. Take a few deep breaths if that helps, laugh at how silly you feel, roll your eyes at each other, even stick out your tongue if that helps you come into the present. Next, hold your gaze, not firmly, but with love in your eyes, until both of you feel unguarded and relaxed. Then, when one of you feels ready, lean toward the other person and tenderly cup his or her head in the palms of your hands. Hold this position while maintaining eye contact, then allow the person whose head is being held to drop his head into your hands. If the weight of the person's head begins to tire your arms, then communicate, with your hands, that you are going to slowly remove them. Try not to speak unless absolutely necessary. After a few moments, take another deep, soft breath and trade positions. Don't be surprised if tears roll down your face, you feel completely exhausted, or you yearn for more nurturing touch, wanting this exercise to go on forever. This can all be part of connecting with yourself *and* with your partner after being so distracted by the daily grind. One woman described it this way: "Doing this exercise I realized how long it had been since my husband and I had softened enough to feel each other's presence. Tears welled up in both of our eyes. We'd been missing each other."

If you both feel like it, remove your clothes. Lie down or sit up (whichever is more comfortable) and take turns simply cupping or cradling other sensual areas of your bodies. Think of conveying, "I love you," through every touch, and let those words be reflected in the nurturing tenderness of your grasp.

ॐॐॐ

Kissing. For some couples, the thought of kissing can be viewed only in a sexual way. However, kissing can be a nurturing activity in and of itself. How do you feel when you kiss your child? Your cat? Your best friend? First, try doing this exercise from a loving and tender perspective, keeping open to moving into more erotic pleasures after twenty to thirty minutes. Concentrate on specific areas of the body first: ears, eyelids, fingertips, back of the thighs, elbows, behind the knees, palms of the hands, side of the neck, and ankles. Move slowly, giving long, soft kisses—at least twenty kisses for each part of the body. If it helps to put on some adagios or light jazz to slow the pace, by all means do so. Don't rush. Focus exclusively on the quality of the kiss and the love you feel for your beloved. Whoever is receiving the kisses should not feel obligated to reciprocate. Of course, moans and sighs of contentment are fine. But the only requirement is to relax and absorb each delicate and appreciative kiss.

If you want to change places so each of you can be the receiver, do so. However, you might decide to have one person be the nurturer and one the receiver one day, then switch roles the next time. It's up to you. A number of women have commented on the fact that, if they feel completely "given to" by this exercise, knowing their partner is cognizant of their needs, they are much more likely to initiate more passionate and stirring lovemaking. If, after doing the first part of this exercise you feel like expanding into the second phase, by all means go ahead. Let the arousal build as you become more relaxed by planting the same long, wet kisses on each other's lips, genitals, breasts, nipples, and buttocks. Then, the rest is up to you and your partner.

Sensual touch need not become sexual. It's designed to relax and nurture each couple by slowing them down and bringing them into the present moment. It promotes closeness and intimacy. It is touch that transmits love and inner beauty, and it can be complete in and of itself. If you and your partner are aroused by such sensual touch (because, certainly, it is erotic), and it opens you to passionately expressing your love, enjoy the tension and attraction!

৵৵৵

Erotic Touch

Making love can be one of the most fulfilling and joyful experiences we can share with another human being. When we reveal our fullest selves through it, we are imbued with magic; ecstasy fills us and we feel complete. As Anne Morrow Lindbergh so eloquently puts it: "When the heart is flooded with love there is no room in it for fear, for doubt, for hesitation. When each partner loves so completely that he has forgotten to ask himself whether he is loved in return; when he only knows that he loves and is moving to music—then, and then only are two people able to dance perfectly in tune to the same rhythm."

Exercises

Stroking and stimulating. Dr. Lonnie Barbach cites some revealing statistics in her book *For Each Other:* "Gebhard's analysis of Kinsey's research of the 1940s showed that only 7.7 percent of women who regularly spent twenty-one minutes or longer on foreplay *failed* to experience orgasm. Hunt's data, accumulated in the 1970s, showed that most couples spend less time than that." In light of this information, it is no wonder that many women have difficulty reaching orgasm. They are not spending enough time building arousal. Obviously, stroking and stimulating with both the hands and the tongue are important precursors to intercourse for women. For this reason, you and your partner may wish to incorporate the sensual touch exercises into your lovemaking as methods of foreplay.

Here is another exercise inspired by Tantric and Chuluaqui Quodoushka lovemaking practices. It focuses on simultaneously relaxing and stimulating the woman so she can more fully experience sexual pleasure, including orgasm. First, lie down on your back with your legs spread comfortably. You may want to prop one leg up on a soft pillow. Have your partner stroke your forehead and face, slowly moving down toward your breasts, stomach, and vagina. Have him gently place one or two fingers inside your vagina, pressing on the G-spot. If you're not sure where your G-spot is, take some time to experiment. As your partner moves his finger inside your vagina, see which area feels the most pleasureable to you—this is your "G" or "Goddess" spot. While your partner stimulates this area, ask him to gently blow on your stomach and breasts. You might also want him to stroke your breasts with his free hand. As you become more aroused, you can ask him to stimulate your clitoris with his tongue or fingers, letting him bring you to climax. Use this exercise as a basis for exploring fulfilling styles of foreplay for both you and your partner.

꒰ꞋꞋ꒱꒰ꞋꞋ꒱꒰ꞋꞋ꒱

Communication. The importance of good communication for achieving true intimacy and exquisitely fulfilling lovemaking cannot be over-emphasized. In their article "The Redbook Report on Sexual Relationships," Phillip and Lorna Sarrel reported that "the ability to share thoughts and feelings about sex with your partner is the single factor most highly correlated with a good sexual relationship." Obviously, volumes have been written on the topic. But you might want to start with a simple exercise such as this one: take turns telling each other, very specifically, about what you find most pleasurable during lovemaking. Try not to focus on negatives, "I didn't like it when. . . ." Instead say, "I prefer it when . . . ," "I feel the most pleasure when . . . ," "I love it when you . . . ," etc. This can set the stage for more honest, less defensive communication about ways to enhance one another's excitement and joy. It can also open the way for less inhibited exploration and question-asking: "Do you like this?" "Do you feel better when I touch you more softly?" "If I suck gently and move my tongue at the same time, do you feel more open and aroused?" Don't be afraid to be specific. Everyone, including infants, knows exactly what type of touch they enjoy, and they will go to great lengths to communicate their needs. Sexual needs are no different.

Another exercise you and your partner might try is expanding your vocabulary for discussing sex. Instead of speaking about it clinically or flatly, be sensual and erotic. "I love the way you taste." "I can't wait until the kids go to sleep so I can take you in my mouth." "You are so beautiful, my love. Can I be inside of you tonight?"

Nonverbal communication is also great—a passionate kiss in the shower. Touching a breast while standing at the stove, sneaking an aroused hug before the baby-sitter leaves, lying on top of your lover and stroking his lips with your tongue just before the alarm sounds in the morning. These can be brief, yet tantalizing ways to communicate to your partner, "I love you. You are so attractive and sexy to me."

Healing Touch

In today's world, it is not difficult for both men and women to feel battered by the external pressures and conflicts we are continually confronted with: fighting to grab a seat on a commuter train, battling rush-hour traffic, contending with mounting financial concerns, attempting to keep one step ahead of office politics, and making sure our children are safe from violence, to name a few. At times, the stress in our own homes can cause us to feel worn and depleted—bouts with croup keep us up all night, a child is struggling with school, and we are trying to "hold it all together" without any reprieve in sight. Under these conditions, it is easy to see why our sex life may take a back seat. However, as Margo Anand points out in her book *The Art of Sexual Ecstasy*, "The problem has reached such proportions that psychologists have come up with a clinical name for this widespread syndrome—Inhibited Sexual Desire." As a society, we are losing touch with a vital life force—one that is essential for our mental health and emotional, spiritual, and psychological well-being. Yet, it is helpful to remember the words of Louise Thornton in *Touching Fire: Erotic Writings by Women*: "Through allowing ourselves to channel love, sensuality, and the force of life itself, we not only open ourselves to the healing of our individual wounds; we also begin to heal all of life." Touch is an indispensable part of healing.

Exercises

Leaning on each other. Remove your clothes and lean up against a wall (or against a stack of pillows—anything to adequately support your back). Then have the other person sit in your lap or between your legs. Take both arms and wrap them around your partner as he sits in your lap, then slowly and sweetly rock from side to side. A variation of this might be cupping your partner's testicles and having him cup your breasts when it is your turn.

やややや

Holding each other. Take turns holding each other in the same way you would carry a child: head resting on one arm while the legs are supported by the other arm. You can do this in a sitting position or supported by a comfortable armchair or the wall. Allow each person ample time to feel loved and cared for, protected and safe.

やややや

Forming spoons. Lie together in the spoon position. Whoever is in back, place your hands over your partner's heart or abdomen, whatever area feels undernourished or needs healing. Then picture yourself sending loving energy to that person through your hands. Allow enough time for a natural closure to occur, then change roles so each person receives some healing.

やややや

Obstacles to Sexual Expression

It is common for new mothers to feel sexually reticent. Not only are there physical factors such as exhaustion, postpartum blues, and vaginal dryness, but there are other, more psychological impediments: body image and conflicting images of motherhood. Namely, does a mother feel comfortable expressing herself as a sexual being?

Self-Image

A mother's self-image can directly affect the degree to which she is sexually desirous; if she feels beautiful, attractive, and "wanted," then she will be responsive to her partner's advances, and she will initiate lovemaking, temporarily overcoming physical considerations such as fatigue. On the other hand, if she feels fat, plain, and, in more extreme cases, ugly, then she will resist any attempts to be physically close to her partner, partly because she doesn't feel good about herself and partly because she is fearful that her partner may view her in the same light.

I remember a group of mothers standing around talking after a parenting class. Several of the moms announced that they felt incredibly sexy with breasts engorged with milk and tummies as round as the moon. They felt voluptuous. A few other mothers told us they felt attractive only when they were svelte and in good physical shape. Yet, as we spoke further it became clear that only those mothers who could not extend their scope beyond a limited definition of beauty continued to feel unattractive. The feedback and questioning from the group gave each mother an opportunity to view herself from another's perspective. "Do you think the women rendered in great art are unattractive?" "Think about women you admire. Are they all one size and shape?" "Even if you don't fit into your 'skinny clothes' right now, are there other outfits that highlight the radiance in your face?"

Another way to improve body image, we all agreed, was to get some exercise: walking with the stroller, swimming, jogging, and bike riding with baby on the back. Whether our weight was "ideal" or not, we noticed we felt better simply because our muscles firmed up, and the increased cardiovascular work made us feel more vital and alive.

Are Mothers Sexual Beings?

Unfortunately, for some mothers, images of motherhood and

sexuality clash. Perhaps they never thought of their mother as having sexual needs. Or maybe their religious practices severely separated the traits of a mother (usually positive) from those of a sexually active woman (usually negative). These fragmented images fail to take a mother's entire identity into account and can result in a mother feeling conflicted about her own sexuality. In fact, some men also have mixed feelings as they come to terms with the fact that their partner, once viewed as a loving and sexual person, is now in the role of "mother." For example, some men feel uncomfortable sucking or licking their partner's breasts after seeing her feeding their child with them. If you or your partner are having difficulty reconciling images of motherhood with images of women as naturally sensual and sexual, it would be helpful to discuss these feelings and bring them out in the open. This will give both of you the opportunity to explore the origins of these unconscious beliefs and make decisions about ways to alter and overcome them. That way you can feel good about being sexually expressive rather than feeling guilty, awkward, and ashamed. You might pick up a copy of Dr. Joyce Block's book *Motherhood as Metamorphosis*. In it she addressses the many self-images and cultural expectations a woman must come to terms with after she becomes a mother.

Relationship Problems/Communication

Another reason mothers may be less inclined to be sexually and sensually intimate is because of problems with the relationship. Built up anger and resentments can dampen sexual interest. Dissatisfaction with the distribution of family responsibilities can obstruct loving and trusting feelings, thus thwarting sexual involvement. Fortunately, there are many resources available for couples nowadays. Books to improve mutual understanding of male and female differences, especially in relation to communication and perceptions, are on the bestsellers lists for months.

Included in the resource section is a list of books that will inspire you.

Resources:

Books

Anand, Margo. *The Art of Sexual Ecstasy.* New York: Putnam, 1989.

Anand, Margo. *The Art of Sexual Magic.* New York: Putnam, 1995.

Barbach, Lonnie. *Resources for Enhancing Intimacy and the Art of Lovemaking: For Each Other.* New York: Signet, 1984.

DeAngelis, Barbara. *Real Moments for Lovers.* New York: Delacorte Press, 1995.

Dinkmeyer, Don, and Jon Carlson. *Taking Time for Love.* New York: Prentice Hall, 1989.

Dym, Barry, and Michael L. Glenn, M.D. *Couples.* New York: HarperCollins, 1993.

Ellenberg, Daniel, and Judith Bell. *Lovers for Life.* Santa Rosa, CA: Aslan Publishing, 1995.

Gray, John. *Men Are from Mars, Women Are from Venus.* New York: HarperCollins, 1992.

Hendricks, Gay, and Kathlyn Hendricks. *Conscious Loving: The Journey to Co-Commitment.* New York: Bantam Books, 1992.

Lee, Victoria. *Soulful Sex.* Berkeley, CA: Lohan Press, 1966.

Louden, Jennifer. *The Couple's Comfort Book.* San Francisco, CA: HarperCollins, 1995.

Mayer, Anne. *How to Stay Lovers While Still Raising Your Children.* Los Angeles: Price Stern Sloan, 1990.

Tannen, Deborah. *You Just Don't Understand: Women and Men in Conversation.* New York: Ballantine Books, 1990.

Welwood, John. *Love and Awakening: Discovering the Path of Intimate Relationship.* New York: HarperCollins, 1996.

*Videotapes**

The Classic Art of Sensual Massage. (Nude models illustrate how to apply sensual massage strokes to both men and women's bodies.)

Sacred Sex: A Guide to Intimacy and Loving. (Explicit video shows couples Tantric techniques to enhance and prolong lovemaking pleasure through guided imagery, erotic breathing, self-pleasuring, and safe touch.)

*Available through the Video Catalogue (800) 733-2232.

Mystical Mamas

I have a close friend in Colorado who gave birth to her daughter just a couple of weeks before my son Alexander was born. Since we were both dealing with the same phases of motherhood, we used to talk on the phone incessantly during the first year of our children's lives. After all, we were in the midst of navigating unknown territory without a compass to guide us. At times we'd marvel at each other, amazed we were making it through this grueling ordeal of being a new mother. Other times we'd laugh at the absurdity of it all. "Yep," she'd say, "today I walked into my closet by accident, but that was not the funny part. I actually *stayed* in my closet and cried. I watched myself doing this, crying in the closet, and I couldn't believe it!" Instantly, I could relate. Although my closet had no room for me to step into it, I found myself fighting back tears in other, equally absurd places in my home.

Motherhood can become so consuming that we can lose our perspective and become myopic. For a time, the larger world shrinks to the size of our living room. This is why it is imperative to get out of the house. Take your baby swimming with you at the local pool, join a mothers' group (start one if you can't find one in your area), and strike up conversations with other mothers at the park.

At other times we need guidance. We need reassuring words that have personal meaning for us, words that inspire us because they speak straight to our soul, words that circumvent the extraneous details of our lives because they go right to our heart. This is when we need to strike out on a more adventurous path. But what do we do when we *really* need to broaden our outlook? What do we do when we need some ethereal guidance? Who can we call, besides close friends, when we need someone to remind us who we are despite the current chaos we are facing?

Consider pursuing a more transcendental route, especially if the advice you're receiving from others is helpful, but does not quite "hit the nail on the head." Why not speak with someone who can relay reassuring words from your spirit guides? Someone who can give you soothing messages from the angels? The thought of getting a reading by a psychic may be new to you, and you may be skeptical. Or you may be a little unnerved by the thought that a complete stranger can access details about you and your loved ones without ever having met you. These feelings are understandable. In fact, I think it is wise to exercise caution. There are plenty of so-called psychics who are simply in the business of making money. Luckily, you don't have to be a "mystical mama" to appreciate the abilities of the women I have listed. I have worked extensively with Lee Cook for more than ten years, and, although all the information she has given me has not been 100 percent accurate (it is a common misperception that psychics always achieve total accuracy), I always gain incredible insights from her readings. I even cried during my first session because of the gratitude I felt knowing my guides knew me so intimately and loved me so unconditionally. I have referred hundreds of people to her and the word I hear most often from others when describing their session is "profound."

Janice Nelson has a different approach. She works with your astrology chart, yet she goes beyond merely describing your sign. She is very good at creating a full picture of who you are, and she can fill in many details about your life—details only you, or someone close to you, would know.

Both Lee and Janice have a wonderful sense of humor, and they can give helpful suggestions (and often unique ones) for dealing with the current issues you're wrestling with as a new mother and the issues related to your own childhood that tend to resurface when we become parents. Perhaps most important, they can both help you to maintain contact with your core self during a time of tremendous change.

If you decide to speak to Lee or Janice (they both give readings over the phone as well as personal counseling sessions, each for a fee), remember: take what you like and leave the rest. Ultimately, only you can decide what is true for you and what is not. Enjoy!

Resources:
Lee Cook (303) 494-3453
Janice Nelson (904) 373-7647

It's in the Cards

When most of us think of tarot cards, we picture a scene from the movies: a dark-featured, gypsylike woman who has long fingers and a look in her eye that might make you think she'd put a curse on you if you didn't pay her adequately. But tarot cards, medicine decks, and other esoteric systems can provide a welcome perspective. They address both the inner and outer realms, illuminating the deeper currents in our lives. Even if we have only five or ten minutes, we can get a quick dose of wisdom that will cycle through our day when we least expect it, continually turning our thoughts away from mindless chatter and back to ourselves.

Tarot Cards

If you go to a New Age bookstore, a woman's bookstore, or some of the larger chain bookstores, you will find an extensive variety of tarot decks. Some of them strictly adhere to ancient esoteric systems, while others are updated and more eclectic in their approach. Take a few minutes to review each deck. You may be attracted to the drawings on the cards. Certainly, some illustrations will appeal to you more than others. I highly recommend Vicki Noble's "Motherpeace: A Way to the Goddess Through Myth, Art, and Tarot." Ms. Noble's deck combines many of the ancient feminine mysteries with shamanism, native traditions, and feminism.

You may also want to pick a deck according to theme. Recently, tarot cards based on Aboriginal, Native American, and African philosophies have been appearing on bookstore shelves. "Earth Tarot" by Jyoti and David McKie, "Medicine Cards" by Jamie Sams and David Carson, and "Sacred Path Cards" by Jamie Sams are among the new releases of tarot decks in this genre.

How to Use Your Deck

Once you've chosen a deck, you will find instructions for reading the cards inside the package. A complete tarot reading can take about one hour. For this reason, you may want to try another, less time-consuming approach—the single-card draw. If this sounds as if you're about to begin a game of poker, be assured, it's a lot easier and the stakes aren't as high.

Begin by shuffling your deck. Then you can cut the deck and pick up the top card, or you can finger through the cards until you arrive at one you feel drawn to. Or you may want to develop your own method of choosing a card. After becoming familiar with your deck, you may be surprised to discover how certain cards stand out to you and that sometimes these cards convey a message that is especially pertinent to you at the moment.

Pick up the card and take a few moments to look at the symbols pictured. Does anything stand out? Does any part of the illustration have special significance for you? Next, read about the card in the accompanying book. Can you relate to the words? Do they speak to your current situation? Do they reiterate things you've been thinking about? Do they directly address aspects of your life you've been avoiding, or things you've felt you haven't had time for, such as taking care of your-

self, redirecting your efforts toward a specific goal, or letting
go of something that is needlessly tying up your energy?

Perhaps you have a specific question you want to ask.
Before choosing a card, concentrate for a few moments on what
it is you want to know. If the card only partially answers your
question, draw another one. You may want to draw three cards
at one sitting to get a more well-rounded perspective and to
give more information to chew on throughout the course of
the day. Remember, there is no right way to read tarot cards.
If you want to strictly adhere to the written instructions, don't
forget to set aside adequate time.

Angel Cards

Angels have been receiving a lot of press lately, and it's a good
thing, too. Otherwise, we would be inundated with little else
but the tragedies and crises of the world. It's nice to have a
dose of inspiration now and then, and that is exactly what angel
cards can provide. The original angel cards are small two-
inch-long cards. One side of the card has an outline drawing
of a tiny angel, and the other side has a word such as "love,"
"humor," "faith," "adventure," "creativity," or "compassion."
The simplicity of the words along with the colorful illustrations surrounding them provide a moment to pause and reflect.
They are a small but simple reminder to "stop and smell the
roses" during the day's confusion. You might want to keep
these cards in a special container on your dresser and take a
minute in your morning routine to breathe in a word of inspiration. Also, if these cards appeal to you, you may want to try
"Angel Message" cards or "Fairie Messages." For a large deck,
try "Angel Blessings: Cards of Sacred Guidance and Inspiration" by Kimberly Marooney.

If you wish to pursue angels further—many mothers do
regardless of their religious upbringing—there are an abun-

dance of books on the market. They can strengthen your faith in the goodness that surrounds you and restore your belief in miracles. You will find a list of books on this subject at the end of this chapter.

Making Your Own Cards

Speaking with different mothers, I discovered some wonderful ideas for constructing your own deck of cards for spiritual inspiration and soothing meditation. The benefit of doing this is that each card is highly personalized and you can choose words, poems, quotations, and pictures that are especially meaningful for you.

One mother copied down the eloquent and whimsical prose in J. Ruth Gendler's book *The Book of Qualities* and placed cardboard on the back of each page. On the front, she wrote down the name of the quality such as "sensuality," "imagination," "anger," "criticism," "intelligence," etc. (there are 100 qualities listed). She has found this to be a helpful way of getting in touch with her feelings. And, as she tells me, "The qualities remind me of my own humanity. I can take an honest look at my own foibles as well as my strengths without judgment because I realize that we all have these traits; we all feel a gamut of emotions; some are comfortable and others are not."

Another mother cut out pictures from magazines, mostly tranquil nature scenes and photographs of sensual beauty and open expanse, and then made them into a deck of 8 × 10 cards. In the morning (or later in the day, if she was too rushed getting everyone ready for school), she would take several of the cards and place them upright on her bureau, the fireplace mantle, and the kitchen counters. Since the scenes were always changing, her eyes did not become overly accustomed to them, thus the pictures were always fresh among other fixed objects in her home.

One of my favorite ways to construct a deck is to write down quotations from various sources. Use index cards or other ready-made blank cards for speed and convenience. Obviously, you can make this into an elaborate project, or you can simply write down twenty to thirty quotations taken from one source.

You may even want to put together a mixed deck of quotations, pictures, and single-paragraph sayings. Be creative. And be realistic. If you tend to think big—imagining yourself putting together a deck that encompasses every meaningful word you've ever heard or read—consider making one card a day (and try not to feel as if you have to make one card *every* day—this is a calming activity, not a goal-oriented one).

To complete your deck (the number of cards is up to you), you may want to go to a bookstore to see if it sells round or square cloth pouches to hold your cards. Often a variety of choices from exotic embroidered silk to colorful floral patterns are available. Pick one that catches your eye.

Resources:

Burnham, Sophy. *A Book of Angels*. New York: Ballantine, 1990.

Freeman, Eileen Elias. *Angelic Healing: Working with Angels to Heal Your Life*. New York: Warner Books, 1994.

Godwin, Malcolm. *Angels: An Endangered Species*. New York: Simon & Schuster, 1990.

Hauch, Rex, ed. *Angels: Mysterious Messengers*. New York: Ballantine, 1994.

Steiger, Brad. *Angels Over Our Shoulders: Children's Encounters with Heavenly Beings*. New York: Fawcett/Columbine, 1995.

Ordinary Is Extraordinary

There is an expression that says, "Life is nothing but the same damn thing over and over." Certainly, there are moments when we all feel that way. Monotony sets in and, for a while, it takes some effort to look at things from a fresh perspective. A classic example: we take our children to the local park on the same day of the week, at the same time, following the same route. What if one day we invited our partner to join us, asking him to stop at the local deli for sandwiches and salads while we supplied plastic wineglasses and paisley napkins with matching burgundy paper plates, and we had a picnic on the grass? Sometimes even the slightest infusion of something new can alter the usual routine tremendously. Or perhaps a different perspective is needed. What about recording firsts, not only for our children, but for ourselves? Remember how special it was the first time we caught a glimpse of cotton candy, and we had to feel it with our tongue? What about the first time we watched a bird take flight? Or remember running through a field of tall grass, so tall that it tickled our midriff? When we can again see the world through the eyes of a child, the ordinary is quite extraordinary.

Charting Firsts

1. Make a chart of your favorite firsts, whatever you remember from your childhood.
2. Then draw two boxes next to each listed item.
3. When your child experiences any notable first—feeling the first feather against his skin, plunging into his first ocean wave, seeing his first shooting star and making a wish—record the time and date in the box next to the listed item that most closely approximates the event. Then, in the second box, write down your own memories of that same, or similar experience.

If you want to decorate your chart, look for colorful stickers that illustrate the events: wizards, clowns, butterflies, locomotives, seashells, dinosaurs, fairies, dolphins, etc. You might consider attaching some of your child's treasures to the chart, especially if your chart is made of sturdy cardboard. Small stones, fishing lures, dried flowers, pieces of a bird's nest, and marbles are just a few of the items that can be added. Or, you might want to place photographs of your child's firsts on the chart alongside pictures from your own childhood and youth. This way you can share in the joy together and create a bridge that joins you.

Charting a New Course

Many children do not like their mothers to diverge from a routine, especially if it involves driving. The route to school cannot be altered. A trip to Grandma's house must follow the same course. The ritual of buying an ice-cream cone on Sunday afternoons must be done at the same store. However, if you are feeling adventurous (and are prepared for the possibility of initial backlash), try going a different route. Drive through a neighborhood filled with old Victorian homes and antique shops. Swing through Chinatown or the Italian Hill if rush-hour traffic won't prolong the ride home. Ask your children to look out the window for new restaurants. Even if they only spy another fast-food joint, it's a change. Although, you might have more success by briefing them ahead of time: "Keep your eyes open for any restaurants with elephants in the window"; "Do you see strands of garlic inside the windows?"; "Can you find a place that looks like it serves old-fashioned milk shakes?"

Another option is to get lost together. Really. Try it. Let your children give directions. They will love the thought of "almost driving" from the backseat and the spirit of adventure might overtake them. "Okay ladies and gentlemen, shall I take a right or a left at the next traffic light?" "Shall we follow the lake around the city?" "Do you want me to head to Forest Park and once we are past the entry gates, you can direct me to the zoo or the museum or the planetarium by reading the pictures on the signs?"

What about stopping at some unexplored place on the way home from school? Perhaps there's a boutique you've been curious about because it has an outrageous name. Go look inside. You can browse while the children try on hats and belts. Visit a brightly decorated penny-candy shop and give your children one dollar to spend. You might even consider taking your children to the Humane Society "just to look" and pet the animals. If you stop by frequently, the staff might let the kids feed the kittens or rabbits. Once Alexander and I decided to check out a strange chalet-type building tucked in the back of a parking lot. It turned out to be a skating rink that was open year-round despite the temperate California weather. What a find!

Consider driving your children to your office as a surprise outing. This will give them a chance to see where you work, and once inside the building, you will be surprised what aspects of your office impress them: the toilets with pedal flushers, the swivel chairs, large windows placed at dizzying heights over-looking the bay. If you don't work at an office, take them to your latest construction site, the riding stable, or the yarn and needlepoint store where you are the cashier. It may seem mundane to you, but to your children it will be new and different, and it will give them a sense of where you spend your hours while they're at school.

If you frequently play the role of chauffeur for your children's ballet classes, sports events, and school activities, consider going to a nearby copy shop and having awards printed up for everyone, including yourself. For example, if your daughter places first in her swim race, congratulate her with a colorful certificate that has her name on it. Be sure to give awards to her closest team members for their efforts and wins, especially if they carpool with you, so that everyone feels included. Then, give yourself an award for your contribution to her success: driving, encouraging, towel holding, and washing out the chlorine from her nylon swimsuit. I'm sure other mothers who share the driving would be honored to receive this simple, yet thoughtful, token of appreciation. Besides, the act of acknowledging your contributions helps your children recognize that without your consistent support, their accomplishments would be more difficult, if not impossible to achieve.

Turning Obligations into Enjoyment

Every mother has specific ideas about the types of experiences she feels will enrich her children's lives. Some insist on music lessons, others lean more toward teaching their children to respect nature. Along with holiday ceremonies and educational activities, mothers strive to set the stage of life by introducing those interests that reflect their values. If nature is their priority, they make sure their children take rafting trips. If family gatherings are important to them, then they plan picnics and ice-cream socials. If art is their passion, they schedule visits to museums and special exhibits for their children. Certainly, these are important choices that shape a child's world. Whatever they are exposed to is what creates their reality and view of life. But what about the little things? Think of the poignant moments in your childhood: watching snowflakes fall from the sky, writing your name on a frosty window, digging your toes into the sand, having an ice-cream soda on the first day of spring. These simple things can turn obligations into enjoyment and add spice to your life, giving your children special memories of the ordinary. Like the other activities you engage your children in, these simple activities develop character, a sense of humor, and creative ways to keep life interesting. Here is a short list of everyday tasks that can become everyday joys.

Laundry. Everyone does laundry. Why not make it snow in July by letting your children play with a box of detergent flakes?

Grocery shopping. I loved shopping with my father. He always raced through the grocery store with me in the cart, announcing our lead position with the other imaginary carts. If this would violate store policy (or if the store is too crowded), assign your children a nonbreakable grocery item to find and then time them to see how long it takes to pick it out and deliver the item to the cart.

Bedtime. What about turning your child's bed into a magic carpet that can fly to any destination she chooses? Have your child close her eyes while you narrate the imaginary trip. Try improvising instead of planning the magical ride—the more details, the better. "We are now passing over your friend Jenny's house. There she is below us. She is smiling. Look at the amazement in her eyes as she sees us flying. Wave to her as we move into the huge, billowy pink clouds. . . ."

Seasons and holidays. Fill a May basket full of fresh flowers to make your children aware of the coming of spring. Go to a big, green field and look for a four-leaved clover to celebrate your Irish heritage. Buy some fortune cookies to celebrate Chinese New Year or a little figurine of the animal that represents the year your child was born. Buy party poppers to celebrate Independence Day. What about marzipan groundhogs for Groundhog Day?

I love yous. Put a little heart-shaped note in your child's lunch box. Or fold a piece of wrapping paper as though a gift is inside of it, but, instead of a gift, write the words "I love you" inside and tuck this in your child's coat pocket.

There are many other small gestures that can break through the routine and add to your life, as well as your child's. It is sometimes the simple things that create the most poignant moments.

Resources:

Krueger, Caryl Waller. *1001 Things to Do with Your Kids*. Nashville, TN: Abingdon Press, 1988.

Nelson, Gertrud Mueller. *To Dance with God: Family Ritual and Community Celebration*. Mahwah, NJ: Paulist Press, 1986.

Unbirthdays

"I cried on my son's first birthday. I cried because he had reached a landmark in his growth. Then I cried because I suddenly realized that I had made it through the first year of motherhood."

Trish, new mother

Birthdays are significant. Like holidays, they serve as landmarks of our growth. They invite us to stop and reflect on the year that has passed. They invite us to absorb the changes we've witnessed in ourselves and to bring them more clearly into focus. Often, emotions we "haven't had time for" suddenly surface, and, for many of us, this is the first time we have allowed ourselves to feel the magnitude of changes that have taken place since we became mothers. Yet celebrations such as these need not be planned occasions. Remember the extravagant tea party held by the White Rabbit and the Mad Hatter in *Alice in Wonderland*? Remember their very merry "unbirthday" song?

In other cultures, celebrations take place when there is cause for celebration. Marlo Morgan writes about the Real People of Australia, who have parties not for birthdays but to recognize one's contribution to life. "They believe the purpose for the passage of time is to allow a person to become better, wiser, to express more and more of one's beingness. So if you are a better person this year than last, and only you know that for certain, then you call for the party."

How many of us have been seized by moments of amazement, joy, and even compassion when we realize how involved we've been in our child's life and how all-consuming our involvement has been? How many of us have taken the time to say to ourselves, "Look what I've been through this year?! I don't know how I did it, but I did it!" Have we taken the time to record our own accomplishments in addition to our baby's? Have we taken the time to think about the ways in which we are better and wiser. Have we taken the time to honor *our* uniqueness?

Birthdays and Half Birthdays

In my family, birthdays and half birthdays were always celebrated—a year between parties was too long to wait. Besides, a good deal could happen in six months. During some years, the changes were so numerous, it seems we could have celebrated every other day. Motherhood is no different. We sail through a flurry of changes, and although it is impossible to be cognizant of every passage, some are simply too important to miss.

Here is a list of a few activities you might try to help you mark these passages.

Send a card to yourself. First, find a blank card with a painting or photograph on the front—something that catches your eye. Next, write a letter to yourself using the same tone you would use to write to your child, recording all that your child's presence has brought you. Then consider what your child would write about you. How would your child describe you?

What attributes and talents would he be thankful for? What would your child say you offered him, simply by virtue of who you are? What would he think is special about you? In what ways would your child think you have grown and changed? What new wisdom have you acquired?

When you're ready, write these things down. Be sure to commend yourself for the ways you've grown and matured, and for your success in handling a variety of new situations. Focus on what you've done right instead of on your shortcomings (unless you can do so with loving compassion). Basically, write a mothering letter to yourself. Celebrate who you are on paper. Then mail your letter to yourself. When you receive it in a day or two many of the words will seem fresh to you. And you may be surprised by what you have written.

Write a poem or two in honor of who you are. Remember haiku poetry from the Japanese tradition? Haiku are always brief but at the same time often rich and full. A few lines bring feelings, passions, and scenic wonders to life. Technically, this unrhymed verse form consists of three lines containing five, seven, and five syllables, respectively. The decision of whether to strictly follow the haiku format or to simply use it as a starting point is up to you. The object is to capture the essence of your experience, as well as the essence of who you are in a few simple words.

At first it may not be easy to distill all of your thoughts and emotions and the events of the past year into a few sentences. Take a few moments to relax. See what images, words, sounds, smells, and touches come to mind. That's the power of poetry—it need not be wordy to effectively communicate an experience, even something as multifaceted as motherhood.

You may want to fill a notecard with haiku, each relating to a different aspect of who you are and what you've come to know about yourself as an individual and as a mother. When you have completed the card, stamp it and send it to yourself.

Write down five to seven answers to the question: What is a gift I would wish to give myself and why? You might answer, "One of the most special gifts I could give myself is a daylong visit to a museum. Why? Because art stirs my soul. I want to be drenched in images. The brilliance of the master painters inspires me; the beauty animates my senses."

Write out as many "wishes" as you like. They can be simple and realistic, or pure fantasy—you decide. Then, send your wish list to your partner or a friend and ask them to grant one of your wishes. Or make your wishes come true yourself (for example, arrange for child care so you can go out and create the rest of your wish).

After you re-read your answers, you will see strands of who you are. Those that link you to your past (life-before-baby) will become apparent, as will the ways that you have changed. Often the image of "a new you" will emerge because, in addition to that part of you that existed before your child was born, motherhood has brought forth many new dimensions of who you are now.

Baby's Birthday

A child's first birthday is certainly an important one. It is one of many firsts we will go through as new mothers. Even if we have a second or third child, firsts are still firsts. It's a cause for celebration for us, too. Enjoy it.

Consider, for your child's birthday, giving yourself the gift of simplicity. Is it really necessary to spend hours writing out party invitations, decorating the house, baking a cake, buying film, charging the video camera battery, and wrapping presents? Why not delegate? If the number of children attending the party exceeds your child's age, ask the other mothers to provide snacks, drinks, cups, candles, and napkins. Also, keep in mind the fact that birthdays frighten many young children. Why not save your energy for when your child is older. Besides, a child who is unaccustomed to lavish parties won't be likely to expect them later on.

Keep it simple by preventing the sole focus from being on material possessions. Have you ever thought of composing a letter to your child, telling her how great you think she is? Even one-year-olds enjoy being read to, though the meaning of each word may elude them. Trust that your voice will adequately convey the very personal message you intend to be heard. This can be a present you give over and over.

Extend the celebration so everyone's expectations aren't hanging on that *one* day. As more seasoned veterans know, the more pressure exerted in the direction of planning fun, the greater the likelihood of a disaster. You might try giving one gift a day for several days in a row. Certainly, a one-year-old won't mind, and toddlers tend to do well with this method as it prevents sensory overload. Older children feel special when you "work up to their birthday" by counting down the days on a calendar. The anticipation is half the fun. Like an Advent calendar at Christmas, you might give very small gifts during the days preceding the big day. Then, on your child's birthday give two or three more significant or special presents.

Last, be sure to have a piece of cake and blow out your own candle. (If you're dieting, pick up a piece of fat-free cake at your local specialty store.) This is a significant moment for you, too. After the hoopla has subsided, take some time, even if it's only a few minutes, to reflect on how far you've come in a year; to examine how well you've juggled competing demands; and to feel who you are, right now, at this singular moment in time. If you give yourself your due, chances are, you will be in awe. Congratulations!

Resources:

Lansky, Betty. *Birthday Parties: Best Party Tips and Ideas.* Deephaven, MN: Bookpeddlers, 1995.

Moore, Thomas. *Re-Enchantment of Everyday Life.* New York: HarperCollins, 1996.

Morgan, Marlo. *Mutant Message Down Under.* New York: HarperCollins, 1994.

Rooyackers, Paul. *101 Dance Games for Children.* Alameda, CA: Hunter House, 1996.

Treasury of Talents

In *Mutant Message Down Under*, author Marlo Morgan writes about her travels with an Aboriginal tribe in the Australian outback. What began as a "visit" quickly turned into a personal odyssey. Like a woman's entry into motherhood, her world was drastically altered in a matter of minutes, and, undoubtedly, the impact on her life would never end. During her time with these so-called primitive people, her perceptions of the world changed. Life as she had formerly known it ended, and as her belief system expanded, she began to think in new ways.

Throughout her book she describes the Real People's thoughts on personal evolution. Unlike Westerners who tend to think in linear terms, these Aboriginals view change as natural to the human organism. They think it is normal to have many different identities in the course of one's life. Moreover, they are perplexed and saddened by the fact that Westerners often avoid pursuing their natural, God-given talents, and that some people never discover their innate worth and thus lead unfulfilled lives. The Real People recognize that each of us has many gifts and skills that can be utilized at different junctures in our lives. And, according to Ms. Morgan, all of these talents seem to be regarded as equally valuable. For example, in her book Morgan described one woman in the tribe as a particularly good listener; her "talent, or medicine, in life was being a listener. Her name was Secret Keeper. No matter what anyone wanted to talk about, get off their chest, confess, or vent, she was always available." If an individual had an innate ability for music, healing, teaching, storytelling, or anything else, then he was encouraged to express his talent, develop it, and offer his services to the group. By the same token, whenever an individual decided to offer another one of his talents to the group, or if his talent progressed to a higher level of mastery, then he might take on a new name to signify this change.

Think how different it would be if we lived in a society that genuinely respected and celebrated everyone's gifts and talents and encouraged their expression—all of them, not just a few. Think how different it would be if financial concerns did not have to be the determining factor for many of our lives. What vocation would you have chosen? How would your life be different? What aspects of yourself would you express more frequently than you do now? Or, if you have pursued your passions, do they continue to be fulfilling? Do you feel others value your talents at home as well as at the workplace? Are there other gifts you possess that you would like to explore, and possibly make a career out of?

For mothers, it is easy to feel as if we put ourselves "on the shelf," or at least a good part of us on the shelf. So often, our needs become secondary to those of others. For this reason, many of our talents may remain dormant. We "forget" aspects of ourselves exist and we minimize their importance. "I don't really need to go horseback riding even though I loved it as a girl. Besides, who has time anymore?" Perhaps we tell ourselves that these things, whatever they are—writing, cooking, drawing, listening, problem-solving, brainstorming, painting, acting, dancing, discussing movies—don't really mean that much to us. We may also talk ourselves out of trying new things and expressing ourselves in ways we have always wanted to. "I'm too old to learn how to scuba dive. Besides, we don't live anywhere near an ocean." If a friend said these very words to you, would you dissuade her or encourage her to get in the pool?

If you find yourself negating parts of who you are and discounting how much certain things mean to you, especially when they seem to call out for your attention, maybe you need to take a second look. Are you dreaming about activities that used to bring you tremendous joy? Do you find yourself thinking about things you love to do, things that give you inner satisfaction and a deeper sense of self, but never making a move toward actualizing them? Do they seem impractical now? Out of reach?

Treasure Chest Full of Talents

The purpose of this project is to lay forth, both visually and with the written word, a mosaic of the various components of who you are past and present, and who you would like to become. It is a way to help you move into the fullness of who you are, as well as embrace who you have always been (including those aspects of yourself that you carry with you even if you no longer choose to express them outwardly—at least not in an obvious way).

1. Collect a stack of magazines that covers everything from fashion to photojournalism. (Choose only those magazines you are willing to dismember.)
2. Lay out the magazines you have chosen. Thumb through them, looking for pictures that reflect your life or the interests you currently hold (these interests need not be new).
3. Separate these images into categories of who you are. For example, if you enjoy nature, and especially like hiking, river rafting, or any other outdoor activity, place all the pictures

you think represent this aspect of you and your interests into one pile. (Don't worry about the number of pictures you've collected.)

4. Sort through each pile. Are there any special aspects of your life that are not represented? If so, see if you can find some additional pictures that correspond to those interests. Or, if time is limited, make a note to yourself to come back to it. Next, pick out your favorite four or five images from each area of interest (depending on their size, you may want to reduce the number of pictures when you get to the next step).

5. Cut out ten to twelve 8 × 10 cardboard cards. Then arrange the pictures in a way that pleases you and glue them to one side of the cards. After you have completed each collage, set it aside until all aspects of your pictorial autobiography are completed.

6. Once the glue has dried, look at the assortment of images you have put together. Study each card, then write four or five sentences about the different aspects of yourself on a piece of colored paper. Be as poetic as you'd like. If you feel stuck, you can begin with: "When I think of myself in nature, I think of. . . ." Perhaps you will highlight your strengths: "I think of how comfortable I feel when I row, and the ways in which I can read the river and anticipate its movements. I feel a sense of connection and belonging." Notice that some cards will be easy to write while others may elicit a more ambivalent and mixed response. Some aspects of your life as represented by the cards may cause you to pause. "Who am I as a teacher?" "Who am I as a woman?" "How do I describe this aspect of myself or my life?" "What exactly is its significance for me?" Remember, there is no right or wrong answer.

7. You may want to place decorations around the words: a strip of patterned cloth, lace, dried flowers, whatever suits you.

Last, make a beautiful box to store them in—this is your treasure chest of talents. Even if you are not currently using all of them to their fullest potential, they are within you and always with you. Isn't it wonderful to see how many talents you possess?

8. Next, make a collage of your dreams—who you wish to become. Don't limit yourself. If you have always wished you could be a famous ballerina, fine. Put her on paper (or find pictures that represent dance to you). Make sure she has her place among your wishes. Don't forget, dreams, fully attainable or not, sustain us and elevate our lives.

9. On a separate piece of paper, make a list of talents that you use for each aspect of who you are. It is important to jot down those intangible attributes such as "patience," "intuition," "compassionate heart," "agile mind," along with your obvious talents such as cooking, accounting, organizing, and researching, etc.

If you are like most women, you will discover you have a multiplicity of talents. You are a jill-of-many-trades and good at all of them. If you are an artist, could you just as easily have been an attorney if you had had the inclination? If you are an avid reader, could you have applied these skills toward journalism? The point is not whether you have had the necessary training or schooling for every talent you possess, but to take an honest look at how valuable each aspect of who you are is, and to remember that each one of these talents could have been utilized in a variety of ways. And they still can be channeled into new directions. For example, you may be a compassionate and able problem-solver who enjoys listening to others. The obvious choice might be to become a therapist. But remember, these talents could also make a great mother or mediator or television interviewer—or, simply, a good person. Again, don't limit your thinking.

Expressing Your Talents

In my work with women, I find that many of the mothers want to expand the expression of their talents. They want to branch out. For some, this means altering their lifestyle. If they stayed at home with their children during their early years, they may want to begin working part-time as their children enter kindergarten. Or perhaps they have decided to return to the local university to complete a degree program. Others volunteer for a certain number of hours during the week for an organization they respect to get firsthand experience in an area they might like to pursue.

Still others prefer to explore areas of personal and spiritual growth by attending workshops, taking trips to exotic places, or involving themselves in activities that may not have had the same appeal just a few years earlier.

Applying Your Treasury of Talents

Once you begin to zero in on your individual gifts—your "strong points"—you can contemplate different ways of applying these talents to benefit you (emotionally, spiritually, and, if you so choose, financially).

Exercise

Take fifteen or twenty minutes and jot down skills and talents that others have remarked about. It could be anyone from a store clerk to a special teacher who sent your poetry assignment home with an "E" for Exceptional. Then, write down whether you appreciated their words, thought they were true, and felt that the compliment validated your own perceptions of yourself. Or did you discount the compliment, dismiss it entirely, misunderstand its significance at the time, or simply fail to comprehend the level of your talent at that particular juncture of your life?

Now, compare this list with your treasure chest full of talents. Are any of these particular talents represented? Then ask yourself, did others' acknowledgments contribute to your better understanding the talents you had to offer? Did you already have a sense of these talents, and others' recognition only helped to bolster your confidence? Did you feel supported by others for your individual strengths? Were you consistently encouraged to express your innate skills? Did the encouragement wax and wane?

ひ ひ ひ

It is helpful to explore which talents or attributes or gifts were encouraged and which ones may have been dismissed (by you or others) to get a clearer picture of why you made certain life choices. Are there any goals you left unmet? Any talents that you would have liked to express more fully? Think big. Think small. It makes no difference. The point is, do you want to express those talents more often in the future, and to what degree?

Now, think about the different levels and possibilities of applying your talents:

1. **Occasional dose of fulfilling personal activities.** These are interests and activities that utilize specific talents such as drawing for pleasure, horseback riding, attending a poetry reading, but the application of these talents is secondary to the sheer pleasure you feel just by engaging in these pursuits.

2. **Regular infusion of passions and interests.** These activities involve a more regular commitment on your part. They may include those interests and activities listed in item number 1, yet you may decide that you need to engage in

them on a more constant basis. In other words, you may feel
that an essential part of your enjoyment of these activities
must include excelling in your mastery of them or being able
to weave them into your life so that they will "feed" you
and utilize your talents in a way that makes you feel good
about yourself. Generally, any achievements gained, besides
the pure pleasures of engaging in these activities, tend to be
of a more personal nature.

3. **Your talents translated into a fulfilling vocation.** These
   types of activities include classes and workshops, internships,
   and a study of topics that are directly related to the talents
   you enjoy expressing the most. Although initially, they may
   not be organized as formal "career plans," they contribute
   to who you are and, eventually, you could apply them toward
   a vocation. It is important to trust that even if you can't
   immediately make the connection, these activities will augment your talents in direct and indirect ways, allowing you
   more flexibility and originality in the future. For example,
   I know one mother who is a registered nurse. She is in the
   process of changing careers to become a massage therapist.
   When a class in astrology was offered by a woman she
   respected, she enrolled. She had always been interested in the
   topic and thought she would enjoy it. At the time, it seemed
   completely unrelated to her future goal. However, the things
   she learned in her astrology class helped her to approach massage therapy in a unique way. In fact, it enabled her to better understand her innate talents and to see ways in which
   she could apply these talents to her chosen field. When she
   eventually did apply to massage schools, she could more
   clearly choose among the various styles of massage therapy,
   thereby focusing in on what she loved more quickly.

4. **Your talents translated into a job description.** These activities vary significantly depending on the job or career you
   have chosen to put your talents toward. If you want to go

into genetic research, certainly that will be different than pursuing a modeling career. Refer to the resource list I have provided to get at the nitty gritty of job searching. Make choices reflecting the best parts of yourself—the talents you enjoy expressing the most—and success will be yours. You have a treasury of talents, valuable and worthwhile talents, that deserve to be shared in whatever forum you decide is appropriate to you.

Suggestions

If, after making your treasure chest of talents, you want to explore new options for applying these talents, expanding these talents, and, possibly, unearthing some new ones, you might try one of these suggestions.

- Contact the author of a book that inspired you. Write to the author in care of the publisher and find out if the author offers workshops, seminars, or group retreats.
- Explore what is offered at your local universities, colleges, community groups and organizations, churches, YMCAs and YWCAs, and continuing education programs.
- Find local newspapers, community papers, and other free publications that offer information on everything from New Age crystal healing to careers in radio voice-overs.
- Find out if there is a reputable and knowledgeable career information center available in your community. Make an appointment. They can offer you some informative tests such as the Myers-Briggs test to help you think of possible applications of your talents.
- Don't be discouraged if everyone around you tells you that you would make the perfect accountant, financial analyst, restaurant owner, or whatever, and you have absolutely no interest. Perhaps you are choosing to develop gifts that are less obvious to the general public. Trust your heart, soul, and passions and pursue what you like, step by step. Unless you

have immediate financial concerns, which you certainly cannot discount, you have time to focus and pull everything together until the moment is right. (As a mother, your own timing may need to coincide with your children's schedules.)

• Believe in yourself. Whatever talents you choose to pursue at whatever level, know that they contribute to who you are. Likewise, what you bring to these activities, interests, and vocations contributes to others.

Resources:

Fox, Matthew. *The Reinvention of Work: A New Vision of Livelihood for Our Time.* San Francisco, CA: HarperCollins, 1994.

Sinetar, Marsha. *Do What You Love, the Money Will Follow.* New York: Dell Publishing, 1989.

Tieger, Paul D., and Barbara Barron-Tieger. *Do What You Are: Discover the Perfect Career for You Through the Secrets of Personality Type.* New York: Little, Brown and Company, 1992.

Creative Expression

In college I was fortunate enough to take a photography class from a young, rather enlightened professor. As part of the course, we were assigned the task of going to the art library and browsing through the works of various artists. The variation in styles was incredible! Although every photographer used basically the same medium, their approach and subject matter contrasted sharply.

During class, we spent many hours examining the photographs and discussing the artists' approaches to their subjects, their use of the camera, the types of film they used, their use of light and so on. Then, to my surprise, our professor announced that we were going to watch several interviews with contemporary photographers. A woman named Judy Dater was among them. When she spoke of her work, she talked about her art not as "something she did," but as who she was. Clearly, being a photographer was an expression of who she was. Sitting in a kitchen with a group of friends who, it seemed, were also artists, Ms. Dater discussed very candidly the challenges inherent in being "a creative person." In fact, as I was to discover, Ms. Dater had an entire body of work, a visual portrayal, that addressed the dilemma mothers have come to know so well: balancing work, especially creative work, with raising a family.

Her words struck a chord in me because, deep down, I knew that even with a degree in international relations, I was not destined to hold a job with regular work hours.

Creativity

Creativity means different things to different people. For some of us it may mean trying a new recipe or organizing a holiday banquet; for others it may mean writing a screenplay or producing a film. Lynn Andrews, author of *Medicine Woman*, once said that there are two kinds of mothers: "Earth" mothers and "Rainbow" mothers. Earth mothers usually channel their creative energy into their family through more traditional talents such as cooking, sewing, organizing activities, and tending to the needs of others. They pride themselves on being available to others. Rainbow mothers, on the other hand, find it essential to incorporate their creative endeavors with the needs of their family. Time devoted solely to their creative expression is essential for them.

No matter what category you fall into, or maybe you're somewhere in between the two, there is no doubt that creativity is important to all of us. Creative expression feeds our spirit and infuses our lives with joy and meaning. Now, for mothers who are able to derive their creative pleasure from baking cookies, organizing fundraisers for their children's school, redecorating their homes, or anything that dovetails with the duties of being a parent, creative outlets are readily available. However, for those mothers who derive their creative pleasure from activities other than those in the domestic arena, finding outlets can be challenging.

Rainbow Mothers and Semi-Rainbow Mothers

Author Toni Morrison once said, "We are traditionally rather proud of ourselves for having slipped work in there between the domestic chores and obligations. I'm not sure we deserve such big A-pluses for that." The fact is, if we thrive on our creativity and the mode of our expression lies outside the domestic arena, it is essential to our well-being to dedicate time to painting, writing, drawing, sculpting, filming, or whatever else stimulates us. Otherwise, we are doing a disservice to ourselves, as well as to those around us by thwarting our talents and casting them aside whenever external demands arise (which for a mother, is often). Always supplanting our creative needs for the needs of others cuts us off from a vital life force and, eventually, leads to resentment, depression, and anger.

Ironically, many of us who are Rainbow Mothers or Semi-Rainbow Mothers, trick ourselves into believing that we can live without our artistic passions, only to find that we lose a certain zest for life. We feel bogged down. Our enthusiasm (from the Greek, "filled with God") dwindles. As Julia Cameron, author of *The Artist's Way*, so aptly puts it: "Enthusiasm is not an emotional state. It is a spiritual commitment, a loving surrender to our creative process, a loving recognition of all the creativity around us." Once we recognize the importance of our creativity and place it in its proper position in our lives, then we can begin to draw strength and joy from it. Tending to our creative process can become one of the single most nourishing things we do for ourselves.

The Needs of an Artist

When we think of what it means to be an artist, how many of us envision someone who is completely free from the obligations of motherhood? How many of us picture an individual with excessive behaviors and an erratic temperament? How many of us say to ourselves, "When I think of who would be an artist, I'm the last person I would think of." As mothers, it is easy to envision the life of an artist and the life of a mother as two mutually exclusive lifestyles. But, they need not be.

Traditional traps. If you believe that the only type of "good" mother is one who is a clone of June Cleaver, then it is very difficult to set aside time for your individual needs simply because June Cleaver, by all accounts, didn't have any. Ask yourself these questions:

- Does the conventional style of mothering fit me?
- Do I find a traditional role satisfying?
- Am I waiting until my children are grown before I make time for my creative endeavors?
- Am I channeling all my creative energy into my children? If so, does this fulfill my creative needs?
- Do I feel selfish if I assert my own needs instead of tending only to those of my family?
- Is it possible for a creative mother to be a good mother?

Nothing can kill your creative flow like guilt. The pressure to be the "good" mother is widespread in our society. And, unfortunately, to the detriment of many, we have a narrow definition of what constitutes a "good mother." Jennifer Louden sums it up nicely in *The Pregnant Woman's Comfort Book*, saying that mothers strive to be everything they think of as good—kind, generous, loving—and feel guilty when they think they've made mistakes. "This kind of guilt signals where you need to grow as a mother, is short-lived, and is healthy. But the daily, energy-sapping guilt that plagues so many of us is damaging, unproductive, and fueled by this culturally engineered myth of the perfect mother."

Artistic women can be particularly susceptible to images of the perfect mother because healthy, admirable role models are often hard to find. It's not that they don't exist, it's just that creative women have often been portrayed as "radical" women who opted to not have a family because of conflicting demands. More recently, images of superwomen who appear to juggle motherhood and creative pursuits effortlessly have become the standard. As Leslie M. McIntyre writes: "Nobody objects to a woman being a good writer or sculptor or geneticist if at the same time she manages to be a good wife, good mother, good-looking, good-tempered, well-groomed, and unaggressive." Exhausting, isn't it? It's enough to make you throw in the towel before you've begun.

Obliterating these stereotypes and erasing images of the perfect mother from our psyches is not always easy. It takes courage to debunk the myth that there is only one "good" style of mothering. It takes courage to design a life that takes your family *and* your creative expression seriously. Fortunately, it can be done.

Step by Step

Take a moment to jot down any mothers you know whom you consider to be especially creative. They need not be "classic artist types." What about someone who teaches elementary school in a colorful way? She always seems to bring in exciting and unique projects for the children. Don't forget the mother who sells real estate by day but manages to paint whimsical children's furniture by night.

Now, think about how these women structure their day or their week. Do they rely on grandparents for child care? Do they enlist their spouses? Have they arranged their studios or a room in the house so that they can watch their children while they work, if necessary? Do they structure their time? Do they plan ahead? Do they work into the wee hours of the morning to follow the muse? If you don't know, ask them. Find out how they handle variables. This will help you to get an idea of the composition of their lives so you can begin to envision new possibilities for structuring your own creative time. Last, find out how motherhood has contributed to their creative talents. Has being a mother helped them to focus? Has motherhood encouraged them to explore new directions? Conversely, how have their creative talents added to their experience of motherhood?

After speaking with these mothers, ask yourself what aspects of their lives might fit you. In what ways do you identify with them? Do you think of them as good mothers? Would you feel comfortable making some of the changes they have made? Do they seem feasible? How could you modify these changes in such a way as to fit your individual needs? In her book *The Artist's Way*, Julia Cameron discusses what she calls the "virtue trap." She writes: "For many creatives, the belief that they must be nice and worry about what will happen with their friends, family, mate if they dare to do what they really want constitutes a powerful reason for non-action." Unfortunately, mothers are prime targets for taking the bait and ending up in the "virtue trap." Face it, you feel guilty when your children are clamoring for your attention, and all you want to do is be left alone (especially if you want to be left alone in your studio). They tell you you are neglecting them. And you feel like you *are* neglecting them. The "good mother" myth is afoot, sabotaging your creative efforts. So, you often end up in scenarios such as this one:

> A woman with two small children wants to take a mask-making class. It conflicts with some of her daughter's ballet lessons, and she wouldn't be able to supply the encouraging nods and smiles. She cancels her mask-making class and plays the good mother, only to find herself seething with resentment on the inside.

Ask yourself: Do I tend to sacrifice my creative desires for the desires of others? Would I feel comfortable attending only some of my children's school and sports functions? Or do I feel obligated to be present at every event? Would I feel comfortable trading off with other mothers? With my partner? Take a moment to think about how often you defer your needs, especially your creative needs, to others. Is there a better way to make sure *everyone's* needs are taken into account, including yours?

Take a look at the "Treasury of Talents" chapter. Think about the placement of your creative endeavors within the scheme of your life. Do you need an occasional creative project, a weekly or monthly dose on a regular basis, or do you feel compelled to vigorously pursue your creative talents? Again, think about rearranging your family's schedule. Learn to say "no" when necessary. Ask your baby-sitter to run errands for you before she arrives at your house. Ask your partner to drive your child to preschool in the morning.

Then, when you have set aside uninterrupted time, take it. Unplug the phone. Hide your lists. Tell yourself all is well. The world will not collapse if you focus on your creative endeavors for a few hours (or even for a whole day!). It is important to remember another essential aspect to being an artist—your creative process is fueled by downtime. Many of us forget this fact, and instead try to cram our creative projects into our schedules as though they were just one more requirement. This approach can quickly diminish your creative zeal. It can overextend you because, instead of reducing your obligations, you simply attempt to pile your creativity onto everything else. This approach might work for Wonder Woman, but not for most mothers—especially those mothers who value being present to themselves and others, knowing that this will enhance their creativity and make them less likely to plunge headfirst into the virtue trap.

One of the most effective ways to avoid the virtue trap is to take downtime. This is an essential ingredient for living a creative life. Julia Cameron has this to say about downtime:

> An artist must have downtime, time to do nothing. Defending
> our right to such time takes courage, conviction, and resiliency.
> Such time, space, and quiet will strike our family and friends
> as withdrawal from them. It is.

For an artist, withdrawal is necessary. Without it, the artist in us feels vexed, angry, out of sorts. If such deprivation continues, our artist becomes sullen, depressed, hostile. We eventually become like cornered animals, snarling at our family and friends to leave us alone and stop making unreasonable demands.

We are the ones making unreasonable demands. We expect our artist to be able to function without giving it what it needs to do so. An artist requires the upkeep of creative solitude. An artist requires the healing of alone time. Without this period of recharging, our artist becomes depleted.

What is downtime? It is lying in bed and daydreaming. Soaking in the tub without keeping one ear alert to someone else's movement. Thumbing through the pages of a book, absorbing each word as though it was rain falling softly on your cheeks. Listening to music and becoming the lyrics and the song. Feeling carefree enough to listen to the wind in the leaves. It is those moments when, for even a short period of time, responsibility is suspended and the true cadence of life pulses through your veins. Take a few minutes to think about what downtime is for you. It can be anything, just make sure you devote some time solely to downtime (no intrusions!)—even if you have to cancel other plans. Last, remember, when you lose yourself in your creative project, transcending self-consciousness, you will be renewed and refreshed in the most abundant ways.

Resources:

Books

Bepko, Claudia, and Jo-Ann Krestan. *Singing at the Top of Our Lungs: Women, Love and Creativity.* New York: Harper-Collins, 1993.

Cameron, Julia. *The Artist's Way.* New York: Putnam Publishing Group, 1992.

Cassou, Michell, and Stewart Cubley. *Life, Paint and Passion: Reclaiming the Magic of Spontaneous Expression*. New York: G. P. Putnam's Sons, 1995.

Eikleberry, Carol. *The Career Guide for Creative and Unconventional People*. Berkeley, CA: Ten Speed Press, 1995.

Suggested Reading

Allende, Isabel. *Eva Luna*. New York: Alfred A. Knopf, Inc., 1988.

Sarton, May. *Mrs. Stevens Hears the Mermaids Singing*. New York: W. W. Norton & Company, 1965.

Fantasy Travel

I recently read an article about mothers who continually fantasize about leaving their families. Inside their heads, they plan their escape from Mommyville. It's not that they don't love their children, it is simply their subconscious sending them messages, telling them that they are neglecting themselves and need to take a break. But, as Sonia Taitz' article, "Motherhood Is the One Job You Can Never Quit," notes, ". . . It's surprising how many exhausted moms continue to say they're happy—not angry. Denial is a warning signal."

Denial

Unfortunately, for many of us, admitting our real feelings is too frightening. What if others perceive us as selfish or ungrateful? What if we admit to feeling trapped? Will others think of us as lousy mothers? So we hide our feelings from everyone, including ourselves. The result is we become further and further removed from ourselves, and we become incapable of being the mothers we want to be. We are more easily angered, we rarely laugh, and we cry repeatedly over nothing. We also have a vague sensation that our lives are drifting away from us, yet we have no concrete plans. And we don't have the energy needed to tend to our appearance or to pursue activities we once relished.

What do we do? First of all, we admit our true feelings. We acknowledge that we're not happy—and there doesn't need to be a reason why. No explanations. Why? Because the minute we start explaining ourselves, others become defensive and feel blamed for our feelings, and this only makes matters worse. The little energy we have to take action is defused by our feelings of guilt, and we end up postponing our plans. We allow ourselves to become overwhelmed, and we fall back into the very routine that first boxed us in. Remember, saying we need to take time alone doesn't have to imply that it's someone's fault.

Honesty

I'm always surprised at the number of mothers who refuse to admit they need time to themselves. Instead of thinking of solitude as *time to themselves*, they more often view it as *time away from their families*. The problem with this attitude is that it induces guilt and shame and perpetuates a feeling of victimization. However, if it is too difficult to declare your self-worth out loud, then write a few sentences on a piece of paper, acknowledging it is all right to take a solo vacation, and repeat this over and over like a mantra until it takes hold.

Then, once you've decided you are ready to turn your fantasy, or at least part of it, into reality, calmly let your partner and your children know about your plans. Just don't expect them to be happy for you—big mistake. Even though deep down, they probably want the best for you, their first impulse is to stop you from going. Young children, in particular, demand our full attention, and they can't imagine what they would do without it, even for a day or two. But it is these unrelenting demands that are burning us out. No one, including supermom, can be all-giving, all the time. You're not a bad person because you need time away.

Turning Fantasies into Reality

Take fifteen to twenty minutes to jot down your most vivid and recurring fantasies. Unlike in dream analysis, you need *not* worry about the particulars. Who cares if you are always running away with Brad Pitt or Sean Connery? What does it matter if you jump on an express train to Vienna? Or that you are the featured singer in a band? Indulge yourself. Don't think about the details too much, otherwise you may begin to fear the worst: "Am I unhappy in my marriage?" "Do I really want to leave my family indefinitely?" And so on. Worries such as these will only create additional concerns that something may be wrong with you since you feel like getting away, *by yourself.*

Instead, pay attention to what you feel. It is your feelings that will help you to make an honest assessment of your needs. Don't judge them. Don't interpret them. But *do* put a name to them. What feelings do these fantasy images invoke? A sense of freedom, independence, peace, tranquility, unbridled laughter, youthful exuberance, mystery, spontaneity, romantic tension, spiritual fulfillment, oneness, harmony, suspension. Don't be alarmed if, initially, you want everything, including the moon. This is common, especially if you have been neglecting your needs for longer than should be humanly possible.

As you label your feelings and desires, ask yourself, "Do I really want to be around other people?" "Do I have enough energy to travel by car or plane?" "Would I feel comfortable being alone for any length of time?" Again, be honest with yourself. Take a few deep breaths. Hide out in the bathroom if you need a place to pause and think. Ask yourself what you want and what you can handle. For instance, freedom may be the feeling you most desire. Does that mean you want to be able to do what *you* want by yourself, with your partner, or with a best friend? Do you have the wherewithal to make reservations, pack a suitcase, and arrange for child care? Or could you achieve a sense of freedom by going for a hike? Taking your dog to the beach? Puttering around an empty house? Chances are, if you feel like totally getting away, possibly moving to Tibet or the West Indies, then you would be wise to come up with several escape plans: one for freedom, one for tranquility, one for mystery, or any three (or more) you choose. All this means is that you have been placing too many aspects of yourself on hold, and they are now calling out for your attention. Often simply acknowledging these needs, answering their internal calls by letting yourself know they exist and are valid, changes your psychological outlook and you feel less confined and weighed down.

Be honest about two things: first, which three aspects of yourself are feeling most deprived? And then, what could you really handle right now?

While it is tempting to reflect on past escape hatches—"Just five years ago I could run a 5K race and feel as free as a bird"— life is different now. As much as you may hate to admit it, you're probably more tired now, you're getting less sleep than you used to, you are calling into service your attention and problem-solving skills more often than a flea hops, and you are in need of retreat time. That doesn't mean you can't work back up to former standards; it simply means that *right now, at the present time*, your spirit is trying to get your attention by sending you movie reels of fantasy vacations. And one day you may take one of these vacations, maybe even all of them, but it is essential at this time to take an honest look at whether these escapes would, if lived out, further deplete you, or, to paraphrase Anne Morrow Lindbergh, "refill your creative springs."

Bringing Fantasies Down to Earth

In the above exercise, don't spend a lot of time thinking about how realistic your desires are. The point is to get clear on what aspects of yourself you want to get in touch with and how you want to feel. Then, bring yourself into the present and respect what you can actually handle *now*. The reason for this is to prevent disasters whereby your fatigued mind so longs to escape, that it forgets what is necessary for the body to do on earth. In other words, there are certain constraints you need to be mindful of in order to not disappoint yourself. Otherwise, you may be discouraged from taking time away in the future.

Take twenty to thirty minutes to visualize fantasies that invoke the way you want to feel. Play them out in your mind, including the details. But—and this is very important—don't think of the details as burdensome, but as part of your adventure. In this way you can consider the preparation necessary to take a minivacation; a week-long excursion; or a simple modification of your schedule that allows for visits with friends, hours at the bookstore, or double-features at the movie theater. "Oh, just thinking about all I would need to do to arrange time away, not to mention the cost, is overwhelming," probably means you will do nothing. But, the fact is, if you are continually fantasizing escapes, you are in serious need of one.

When you finally settle on what type of escape would best suit your present circumstances, start planning it. You may be too tired to feel pure, unadulterated enthusiasm, but instead of fretting over the details or the possible problems, trust that things will go well. Believe that the time away will benefit everyone regardless of whether they scream and howl upon your return. They can't help it if their world revolves around you. Take it as a compliment.

Then go. Enjoy yourself. Who knows, some surprise might be in store for you! And you might decide not to run away from your family after all—except on certain occasions.

Sanctuaries

For many of us, our home is our sanctuary. We like nothing better than basking in the peace of an empty house, leisurely moving from one activity to the next: cleaning closets, slumping on the couch with a magazine, or clutching hand to breast as we watch our favorite old film or listen to music from another era. Though they are rare, these times allow us to move with the more natural cadence of life. Like the soothing beat of a steady, calm heart, we move to our own rhythms, not those dictated by the hustle and bustle of the modern world.

While it is important to ask our families occasionally to leave us to our own devices at home, it may not always be feasible. For this reason, we might consider other, equally appealing options where inner rhythms are respected, contemplation is encouraged, and solitude is available. There are many kinds of sanctuaries available: monasteries, abbeys, retreat centers, hermitages, or cabins in the woods.

What Can a Sanctuary Offer?

A sanctuary can offer a lot. As Marcia and Jack Kelly write in their guide to sanctuaries, "Not only is this an opportunity for time apart . . . but a time to reach for our best selves, to think

189

about and practice our best values on a daily basis, then take them back to our 'regular' lives." Besides providing manna, or food, for our souls, retreat centers offer everything from abundant natural surroundings to prayer services, workshops, and hot springs. The settings are diverse as are the residents. Although some of the sanctuaries are administered by a religious order, others are more loosely dedicated to an eclectic variety of spiritual principles. However, this does not mean that participation in any of the services is mandatory. If you want to join in you can, and you will feel welcomed by the spirit of openness and warmth, but it is an individual choice.

Places such as Esalen Institute in Big Sur, California, often have seminars, classes, and workshops, as well as group conferences on topics from a variety of fields and academic disciplines. You may want to contact them well in advance to find out what is being offered, especially for their summer programs, in order to register for programs of interest. (Also, an early reservation will ensure you a space, and many of these retreat centers fill up quickly.)

If you are most interested in being alone, hermitages may be the route to go. On the other hand, if you are eager to try something new, look into those sanctuaries that offer singing, dancing, and drumming. Others, Tassajara Zen Center in Carmel Valley, California, for instance, offer world-renowned vegetarian cuisine, access to mineral hot springs where you can soak and relax, and swimming in the great outdoors (weather permitting).

Expect the unexpected. You never know what you might find, except, perhaps, peace of mind and a sense of self.

Expenses

Fortunately, many retreat centers are moderately priced. They range from $15 to $175 a night. Most places offer meals, while others provide a group kitchen for food preparation. Be sure to inquire about what is included in the fees (meals, access to swimming pools, hot baths, private or shared rooms, and so on). You should have no problem finding something wonderful in your price range. Money need not be a deterring factor.

Resources:

Benson, John. *Transformative Getaways for Spiritual Growth, Self-Discovery, and Holistic Healing.* New York: Henry Holt and Company, 1996.

Burt, Bernard. *Healthy Escapes.* New York: Fodor, 1993.

Kelly, Marcia, and Jack Kelly. *Sanctuaries—The Northeast: A Guide to Lodgings in Monasteries, Abbeys, and Retreats of the United States.* New York: Bell Tower, 1934.

Kelly, Marcia, and Jack Kelly. *Sanctuaries—The West Coast and Southwest.* New York: Bell Tower, 1993.

Car Sanctuaries

The American invention of the car has altered our society dramatically. In the 1950s the automobile provided a place to "make out," giving middle-class teenagers their first glimpse of sexual freedom. In the '60s cars were used for makeshift homes, protest vehicles, and psychedelic art; in the '70s bumper stickers proclaimed the opinions of the driver; and in the '80s the automobile represented status and luxury. Now, in the '90s cars serve just about every purpose imaginable. If we feel as though we live in our cars, it's only because we do. So, why not think of a car as something more than mere transportation. Why not turn it into a sanctuary of sorts?

Tapes and CDs. One mother, Linda, realized that she toted an incredible number of tapes around for her three children to listen to but had long since forgotten about her own musical tastes. "It's not worth the fight," she told me. Then she decided to allot a certain amount of time for each person. One day her eldest son made the music selection, the next day her daughter chose the soundtrack from *The Little Mermaid*. Linda rotated until everyone, including Linda, was able to listen to his or her favorite tunes.

Another mother keeps two cassette cases accessible in her car. When her children ride with her, she will often play music they like or listen to stories with them. However, after delivering her children to school, she switches to more soothing music, preferably music without any lyrics. This helps her to relax and turn her focus to the day ahead of her.

Other moms choose to use their driving time to learn a new language, to have a good book read to them, or to listen to a public radio show they missed (these can be ordered through your National Public Radio local affiliate). This connects them to the "adult world" without overwhelming them with the broadcast news.

One mother I spoke with suggested pulling over to the side of the road, reclining the seat, and listening to tape recordings of ocean waves, the howls of wolves, birdsongs, or other "music" found in nature. "You only need five to ten minutes of this to put you in a more tranquil state of mind. Then you can go home with some new energy for the kids."

What about singing at the top of our lungs? A close friend, who is also a mother, decided to record all her favorite songs from the '60s on one tape. Not only does she know every word to every song, but she discovered that her children enjoy singing along with her. She can share a part of her world with her children or bebop alone, pretending she's performing before cheering crowds and bright stage lights. "Being a mother doesn't mean you have to be dull. It's fun for my children to experience my boisterous side."

Moons and mantras. Many mothers fasten affirmations to their dashboards. That way, when they need a little reassurance or a point of focus, they simply turn their gaze to the words they've written down for inspiration. "I try to change my affirmations on a regular basis. Otherwise, they can fade into the background and are hardly noticed." Other mothers keep a meaningful prayer within view. Still others buy small magnetic words to place on the driving panel. This enables them to create poetic phrases or clever sayings.

Rearview mirrors. I'm sure, like me, you've seen everything from rubber chickens to Native American dream catchers hanging from the rearview mirrors of automobiles. It's like looking in someone's refrigerator—the way a car is adorned reveals a great deal about its owner. Why not make your own statement? A mother of five hangs a beautifully illustrated picture of the Virgin Mary from her rearview mirror so every time she looks into the mirror, she sees kind and compassionate eyes gazing back at her. Some mothers hang pictures of their children or pictures of places that have significance to them. One mother cut out two photographs from a magazine and pasted them on either side of a card. As her car moves, the pictures rotate. Another mother kept a picture of her favorite dog on her mirror.

Camping out. I was surprised by the number of moms who divide their trunk space to allow for a storage section specifically for their driving comforts: pillows, seat covers, blankets for a quick nap in the park. One mother dutifully hides a plush sheepskin seat cover that she only pulls out when she's riding alone. She doesn't want to subject her prized object to mud, gum, and crumbs. Then there are those women who keep a fresh change of clothes, an extra gym bag, books, stationery (to catch up on letter writing while waiting for sons and daughters to emerge from classrooms), and anything else they might need for driving or waiting in the car. I always travel around with a pad of paper and pens to jot down book ideas. Basically, the idea is to keep your car stocked so that you can always take advantage of any spare time that may mysteriously and thankfully arise during the day.

Glove compartment goodies. Glove compartments are made for more than gloves. What about keeping chewable vitamin C tablets or zinc lozenges handy? Keep up your health while driving. There's gum for chewing, or you may want to try some ginseng or real peppermint from your local health-food store. Chocolates are good—perhaps individually wrapped truffles from Europe? (It's the next best thing to bonbons in the bathtub!) Granola bars, calcium bars, and energy bars are all healthful snacks (and you won't mind if your children discover your hiding place). You may even try organic almonds, cashews, pumpkin seeds, or sunflower seeds. In moderation, these can help to curb the symptoms of PMS. Italian biscuits (biscotti) are crunchy and sweet, and although the sugar content is usually low, they're very tasty. Rice crackers now taste like more than cardboard: popcorn, caramel glaze, nacho cheese, or onion and garlic.

Chances are, like most moms, you will be caught in between meals. To maintain your energy and quell your appetite, keep your glove compartment stocked.

Mobile altars. Granted, you have to have the right dashboard design for this, but some mothers are putting mobile altars in their cars. As one mother told me: "I spend more time in my car than at home so, for me, it makes sense to decorate my car with my sacred objects." Feathers, stones, angels, pouches filled with herbs, dried flowers, colorful beads, seashells, ornaments, and goddess figurines are just a few of the items you can use to adorn your vehicle. They are a welcomed contrast to the cold metal of an automobile, and they make you feel at home.

Stars on the ceiling. If you haven't already been introduced to the many glow-in-the-dark items that can be placed on the ceiling, check out what's available. There are stars and planets and moons of all phases—waxing, crescent, and full. Some are large. Others are small. Some have color. Others do not. Have fun with them.

Once you have turned your car into a sanctuary of sorts, use it. On your way home from work, sing and loosen up. Play soothing music to help ease the pressures of the day. Bring closure to your day by sitting in the driveway for a little while and taking some time to catch your breath and regroup (at least until your children spot you). If you've been driving children around all day, give them a chance to run into the house without you, then jot down whatever is on your mind so you can put it to rest, at least temporarily. If your head is swimming from too many demands, let out a few hardy laughs and repeat over and over, "Yes, this is my life," until you can clearly see the humor in it. Or, if you need to, let out a few tears and acknowledge that you're exhausted and happy the day is coming to a close. Soothe yourself by stroking your face, looking into your own eyes (remember the rearview mirror), and telling yourself all is well. Make sure your voice exudes the same confidence and faith you use when you speak to your children. Picture yourself going inside, greeting your family, and changing into comfortable clothes. In other words, prepare a brief "coming home" ritual, playing it over in your mind so you won't be overwhelmed by the chaos of children and pets. Then, when you are ready to leave the sanctuary of your car, go inside. Hopefully, you will be ready to enjoy whatever comes next.

Order and
Going with the Flow

One day while at my son Alexander's school I was speaking with Barbara Rabin, the director of Ananda who also teaches the primary grades. Not only is Barbara responsible for planning the curriculum but, as a teacher, she must also implement the very program she creates. As we were talking, she told me about an elementary schoolteacher, who had once made a memorable comment to her during one of their discussions. "You know," the woman had said somberly and with a touch of irritability, "if it wasn't for the children, my classes would run smoothly." Barbara and I had a good laugh, knowing there can be nothing more annoying and totally delightful than the unpredictability of children. They teach us about honoring internal rhythms and bending to the currents of life even if that does not always coincide with our preplanned schedules. Oblivious to time and always asserting their personalities, they cause us to assess and reassess our blueprints for the day, for the week, for the year. They remind us that life is not lived in one straight line, although we may wish that it was. In short, children do not make life convenient, nor do they cater to what seems to them to be random efficiency. Instead, they teach us about balancing order and "going with the flow."

Several years ago, noted author Mary Catherine Bateson gave a presentation in the San Francisco area. She spoke about women's "peripheral vision"—the ability to hold many levels of awareness simultaneously. Being an anthropologist, she was well-acquainted with women's use of peripheral vision throughout the world. During her talk she related a story about the Bushman tribe, a hunting-gathering people in Africa. As it turns out, women of the tribe gather more than 50 percent more food than their male counterparts regardless of the fact that the women visit with each other, care for children, and tend to other needs of the tribe while foraging for edibles from the desert. As Bateson points out, at first glance the men appear to be more efficient simply because they only have one task to perform—they can remain single-minded. Yet, it is the women, with their ability to tend to many things at once, who actually keep the tribe fed. In Bateson's words: "Women, on the whole, have not had the privilege of single-mindedness. Instead, women have had to learn to be attentive to multiple demands; to think about more than one thing at a time. This skill is absolutely essential in the modern world."

While it is true that women's talent for holding many focuses at once is admirable (many corporations are even adopting this very quality as part of their managerial policy), it is also true that it takes a great deal of energy to continually operate in this mode. In addition, when we are habitually presented with an onslaught of external stimulation (especially those that require a response), whether it be people, products, or noise, we are always directing our attention outward. And if we do not remember to turn our focus inward and shut out the multifocuses vying for our attention, we can become overwhelmed and, ultimately, less effective in juggling the many aspects of our lives.

On the other hand, when we take this multifaceted approach to everyday life and slow it down to normal speed, it is anything but draining. In fact, in this mode of operating, we feel more present to the moment, we can make choices easily, we can move in and out of activities with effortlessness, and we have a profound sense of "flow."

Going with the Flow

Lie down and listen to the crabgrass grow,
the faucet leak, and learn to
leave them so.

Marya Mannes, author, Last Rights

In our busy lives, going with the flow is not easy. Even if we decide to unfetter our day from cares, the telephone rings and demands our attention, bills arrive and require payment, events take place and call for our attendance. It is difficult to say "no" without feeling guilty; it is difficult to say "no" when we are sure there will be reactions. However, as Anne Morrow Lindbergh points out, "Woman's life today is tending toward the state William James describes so well in the German word, 'Zerrissenheit'—torn-to-pieces-hood. She cannot live perpetually in 'Zerrissenheit.' She will be shattered into a thousand pieces. On the contrary, she must consciously encourage those pursuits which oppose the centrifugal forces of today. . . ."

Exercise

Take a day, if you can, or a few hours, to allow yourself to move into the cadence of life, the inner life, that is more in accord with the beating of a heart than the racing of an engine. This can be done alone or with your child (when you are calm, your child will tend to move into your flow, at least for awhile).

First, unplug the phone, turn down your answering machine, leave your letters in the mailbox, tuck your lists away, and take a deep breath. Focus. Is there a place you can find within that feels serene? Even if it is small, find it and focus on it. Most likely, many thoughts will tumble into your head. You will remember all the little things you haven't tended to; you will think of upcoming projects; and you will recall phone calls you forgot to make or stamps you forgot to buy. Promise each of these thoughts you will return to them, then let them go, release them for now. If your thoughts respond anxiously, "You'll never remember all of this!"—write down whatever comes to your mind for five minutes, but only five minutes. If, to avoid creating more worries, you feel the urge to dive into a project, answer a few calls, or write out that thank-you card, tell yourself that today you are gathering the necessary strength to do these activities at a later time. Remind yourself that if you are not inwardly attentive, you will not be able to bring your best to all you hope to accomplish. Then return your focus to what is before you—an open day. Are you growing impatient, feeling that if you do not make plans, there will be no structure, and without structure, you will be without direction? (Most of us do!) If so, try cutting through this thinking and ask yourself, "What do I want to do?" Or, if you are doing this exercise with your child, you may hear, "Let's go outside and plant some seeds." Even if your child's idea doesn't necessarily appeal to you, try moving with it, bringing your attention to it, being present to it, without judging whether you like it or not. Otherwise, this judgment could present an obstacle to whatever may transpire. Instead of saying (either out loud or to yourself) "We'll garden for thirty minutes, then I want to listen to Bill Moyers and Joseph Campbell discussing *The Power of Myth*" (again planning), try watching your child. Unless accustomed to jumping from one activity to another, never fully engaging, you will find that something inside of your child signals when the project is complete. The activity has come full circle, there is closure, and it is time to move on to something else: examining a flower, watching a worm bur-

row in the earth, or catching a ladybug. Notice that the project need not be *finished*—completed and finished are not the
same thing. Now you try it. Be cognizant of your surroundings. Bring yourself to whatever activity you choose—arranging flowers in a vase, listening to music, brushing your hair. If
you feel this exercise is "too Zen for you," remember it need
not be a solemn procedure or a strict practice. The point is to
attend to your present activity and feel when it is completed
(not necesarily finished). Then, move on to something else
when you can feel, viscerally or intuitively, it is time to do so.
This rhythm is called "flow." By transcending temporal restric-
tions, you allow yourself to move with greater ease. You may
discover, as many mothers do, that you are actually *more* efficient with your time and energy, and the quality of your activity is increased.

ॐॐॐ

Some mothers start out doing this exercise one hour a day
until they feel comfortable moving at a pace that neither their
mind chatter, nor the outside world, seems to dictate. Now
your natural pace seems to emerge from feelings or a sense of
"what do I want to do right now?" It's as though ideas that
pop into your mind, in the moment, have already synthesized
what you need (many people refer to this as the innate intelligence of the body and mind), so the choices that are presented are aligned with your true inner need to rest, be alone,
move, relate, listen, pray, laugh, etc. For example, you may have
an awareness that a bath would "hit the spot." Then, when
you've completed your bath time ritual, you feel you'd like to
watch a movie, and buttered popcorn would taste great. Next
you may want to go to a gardening store and browse until you
no longer feel like browsing, and then maybe lie in the grass
because time is irrelevant. Unlike planned activities where we
feel the pressure to cram everything we would like to do into

one day, in a flow state it doesn't matter whether you get to each activity. What matters is that you are receiving inner guidance about the things that would nourish you, and you are remaining present to them so they can actually give you what you need. It's like eating food. Even if you eat the right vegetables, fruits, protein, and so on, they will do you little good if you do not chew them properly and allow your body time to ingest the nutrients.

Eventually, if you become more aware of the moments or times in your life when you feel "flow," you will create more of these opportunities because it is normal for the human organism to want to move at this more natural cadence. And, hopefully, you will find it easier to return to this state regardless of how hurried your day or week has been.

The Importance of Order

On the opposite end of the spectrum or, more accurately, the other side of the same coin, is order. Granted, a certain order can be achieved with flow, yet with so many external demands placed on us, it is essential to create structure. Think of flow as an expanded state and order as a more focused state requiring single-mindedness (even if this means concentrating on one aspect of our life at a time, rather than eliminating all but one focus from our mind). As mothers, we are continually ordering and re-ordering our days as things arise. And, although there is always fluidity in our day owing to our responsibilities for others, it is important to respect our own need for the underpinnings of our life to be in place because they serve as our foundation. Every day we combine flexibility and order. Yet, if we are too flexible, always bending to the demands of others, our foundation weakens and we feel shaky.

Creating Order

Like flow, creating order requires that we turn inward initially in order to gain our equilibrium. Think about it. What rituals help you to feel more orderly? Organizing your kitchen cabinets? Taking your car in for an oil change? Making a list for the upcoming day, week, or year? Cleaning the house? Being able to finish a project from work without interruptions? Do you allow yourself time to focus or do you feel pulled from one activity to the next? If so, you would probably benefit from simply stopping and allowing yourself the space to regroup.

Again, like flow, the drawing together of self can better enable you to deal with the complex demands you must piece together into a cohesive whole. The difference is that order is like a brief pit stop that assists you at rapid speed instead of the expanded movements of flow where time constraints are virtually irrelevant.

Respect your need for order. It is a statement of your boundaries; it is the ability to organize others' schedules; it is the ability to orchestrate life. However, it is essential to remember that order and rigidity are not the same thing. When we become rigid, we constrict, and if we constrict too tightly, we are less able to handle life's many fluctuations. It is during these times that we may make desperate attempts to create external order because, internally, we feel out of control. We may be operating out of an illusion of control, attempting to make life static instead of adjusting to changes and moving with them. Like the elementary schoolteacher Barbara Rabin mentioned who thought it more important that her program run like clockwork rather than alter her plans for serendipity, we, too, can become too attached to order. Why? Usually we do this when we are afraid, or when we feel too stretched to respond to changes. Take a break. Surrender for a moment, just long enough to look inside. If we're feeling afraid, what are we afraid of? Feelings? Standing up for ourselves? Do we feel victimized by somebody or something? Or are we simply too tired to deal with change? Do we feel burned-out and that by constricting our body is saying, "Stop! I've had enough! I've hit *my* limit!" (Which, by the way, may be different from someone else's limit). Respect your personal comfort zone, it is sending you a very clear signal: "Replenish!"

In John Gray's book *Men Are from Mars, Women Are from Venus,* he talks about women's tendency to expand and pull themselves outward when, in reality, they need to gather themselves together. The result, as we all know, is anger and resentment; a feeling of being spread out too thin; a feeling of being taken advantage of. We overemphasize the needs of others at a time when our own soul really needs to be fed. As Anne Morrow Lindbergh so aptly puts it: "Not knowing how to feed the spirit, we try to muffle its demands in distractions. Instead of stilling the center, the axis of the wheel, we add more centrifugal activities to our lives—which tend to throw us off balance."

Ironically, it is often at these times that, in order to create order, we must first stop, pay attention, and go with the flow for a time, until the clarity of our focus returns. Then we can reorder our lives, not simply out of a need for control, but as a way to build a foundation to support the influx of changes that life, especially life with children, will inevitably bring.

Resources:

Books
Ban Breathnach, Sarah. *Simple Abundance: A Daybook of Comfort and Joy.* New York: Warner Books, 1995.

Bateson, Mary Catherine. *Composing A Life*. New York: Penguin Books, 1989.

Cook, Marshall J. *Slow Down and Get More Done*. Chicago: Better Way Books, 1993.

Csikszentmihalyi, Mihaly. *Flow: The Psychology of Optimal Experience*. New York: Harper & Row, 1990.

Hunt, Diana. *The Tao of Time*. New York: Holt Publishers, 1990.

Lindbergh, Anne Morrow. *Gift from the Sea*. New York: Vintage Books, 1978.

Moore, Thomas. *Care of the Soul*. New York: HarperCollins, 1992.

Robinson, Bryan. *Overdoing It: How to Slow Down and Take Care of Yourself*. Deerfield Beach, FL: Health Communications, 1992

Saavedra, Beth Wilson. *Meditations for Mothers of Toddlers*. New York: Workman Publishing, Inc., 1992.

Tapes

Bender, Sue. *Everyday Sacred: A Woman's Journey Home*.
Audio Renaissance Tapes
5858 Wilshire Blvd., Suite 205
Los Angeles, CA 90036

Saavedra, Beth Wilson. *Meditations For New Mothers*.
HarperAudio
10 East 53rd Street
New York, NY 10022

(Tapes can be ordered directly or purchased at bookstores.)

Strategies and
Sanity Measures
for Supermoms

Nancy Crossman, Editorial Director for Contemporary Books, captured the feelings of many mothers when she said: "I love my children and I love my career, and I don't want to compromise on either one. What gets left with little attention?" We all know the answer: "Me." The fact is, many of us are stretched to the maximum, wanting to give our family the very best *and* wanting to excel in our careers because we find our work to be fulfilling, and so it seems there's little room for taking care of ourselves. However, speaking with other professional women who are mothers, I discovered an array of brief, yet life-renewing rituals that can be slipped in between the frantic pace of work and the constant demands of family life. In addition, there are "tricks of the trade" that each of us can benefit from—simple timesaving strategies that can make life run more smoothly.

Morning Routines

Early risers. For those who enjoy sunrises, set your alarm a half hour earlier than usual so you can avoid the crowds. Put on a kettle for a cup of coffee or tea, prepare a simple breakfast (or prepare it the night before), catch up on the news, read that magazine you've been wanting to, or take a few moments to hear yourself think. Then, when it is time to wake up the crew, you'll have had at least a brief respite of solitude.

Late risers. For those of you who need quiet moments of meditation while still horizontal, ask your partner to tend to the early risers (hopefully, he's a morning person). If not, trade off mornings so neither of you is deprived of those essential fifteen to twenty minutes of transition time *every* day. Keep the door closed to muffle the noise and possible distractions, and allow that groggy state to clear like mist over the harbor. This will help prepare you for the day with a clearer, more lucid mind.

Mothers of early risers. Teach your children to prepare their own breakfasts, or designate a certain part of the fridge for breakfast items (yogurt, cream cheese and bagels, fruit, low-fat muffins, etc.). As one mother and attorney told me: "Delegate as soon as you can. It makes things easier for mothers and gives the kids a sense of responsibility." This will allow you extra time in bed or five more minutes in a hot shower so you can concentrate on the schedule for the day. On the other hand, if your children depend on you to wake them and require assistance getting mentally prepared for school, plan to read them a story upon rising (this will give you a few more comfortable moments in bed), get them settled with breakfast, and return to bed for ten to fifteen minutes, especially if your partner can take it from there.

Commuter moms. If you travel by bus or rail to work, be sure to pack a crossword puzzle or needlepoint project in with all your papers to keep you thinking straight. Try carrying note cards with you so you can write to a friend, taking time to focus on your relationships instead of constantly rolling dead-lines over in your mind. One accountant confided: "I deal with numbers all day long. Occasionally, I enjoy reading a trash novel on the train. The contrast is wonderful!" You might also enjoy having a small, family photo album with you. Pull it out when you're feeling overwhelmed by the centrifugal forces of life (yes, even during meetings).

Tools of the trade. Just as an artist needs her paintbrushes, mothers who are also professionals need certain tools. Would a laptop computer assist you so that you wouldn't need to carry all kinds of information around in your head? Do you need several briefcases—one used strictly for work and another that holds other essential items (pull-ups, toys for the ride home from day care, snacks) in addition to papers and calculators? Who cares if you look like a "briefcase lady"? You'll have what you need when it comes time to "change hats." In the evening write a list of the next day's essentials, then follow that list in the morning, making sure you have all the items that are important for the day. Now you won't need to run back home or do without.

Midday Madness

So often, our mornings make us feel like racehorses bolting out of the gate. But, unlike the horses at the track, we continue at breakneck speed until we return home from work. By that time, we're bleary-eyed and ready to collapse. Quality time with our children is hard to muster. What about slowing our-selves down in intervals throughout the day so we can rejuve-nate in short stints? If you're shaking your head and thinking, "There's no way I could manage that with my schedule," think again. Remember, even marathon runners take quick stops for food and water to help sustain their endurance. Here is a list of some quick stops that could help restore your energy.

- Take a brisk walk during your lunch hour.
- If the local library is nearby, take a twenty-minute snooze in one of their stuffed chairs.
- Stretch your arms and legs, neck and shoulders. Use the ladies room if a lounge isn't available.
- Keep some aromatherapy scents in your top desk drawer. Just the sweet smell of orange, jasmine, lemon, pine, ylang-ylang, or sandalwood can bring a weary spirit back to life.
- If you need silence, but cannot leave the building, do what you do at home. Find privacy and quiet in the rest room or another place you can be alone.
- Keep a towel at your office. On a pleasant day go to the park and lie on the grass with the sun on your face for twenty to thirty minutes. (Sunlight is a natural way to fight fatigue and depression.)
- Break up your day with a pottery or African dance class.

Energy at the End of the Day

If possible, take some time for yourself before your children arrive home from day care or school. Here are recommendations from other mothers on the go:

- Skip lunch hour occasionally and come home early to take a nap, listen to enjoyable music, read a novel, or garden before your children come home (or before you pick them up).
- If you arrive home after dark take a few minutes to sit in the car in your driveway before entering your house. Look at the stars, play some music, listen to National Public Radio, breathe, and unwind after the rigors of the day before you say good-bye to your baby-sitter for the day.

- Engage your children in a quality video while you take a hot, scented bath. Then prepare dinner together. As a busy grandmother told me while on a camping trip, "It's only a chore if I'm in a hurry." Use the dinner hour as a calming activity instead of one more chore to complete.

- Have your children change into fresh clothes, and let them sleep in those clothes (dresses might not work) so neither of you will have to bother with picking out an outfit in the morning. Don't laugh, it's tried and true!

- Our family friend, Ruth Kedar, told me about a Yiddish word, *dybbuk*, which roughly means "to be possessed." Being an artist, mother, professor, aikido expert, wife, and exuberant person, Ruth understands that there are times when she is so overtaken by her creative work that her family must fend for themselves. "I'm indisposed," she says, riveted with the muse. There are many ways to handle these times (and all mothers have them!): place a green flag on the refrigerator to signal that you must be relieved from your household duties temporarily. Have an emergency plan for these occasions, such as your partner's contacting the baby-sitter and extending her hours; his cooking dinner or ordering in; his taking over bedtime routines, calling you in only for the last twenty to thirty minutes of book reading and tucking everyone in. Other mothers wear different hats, literally. If the white hat is on it means, "I'm stressed out over this project, but I'll be back to my cheerful self soon." If you think these ideas sound eccentric, think of how you look when major deadlines require temporary alterations in your lifestyle and you're stressing yourself out, trying to act as though it is life-as-usual. Drastic times call for drastic measures. Be creative.

- Keep an enormous monthly calendar on the wall and write each family member's events, appointments, and special dates in designated colors of erasable marker. This way, the left hands will know what the right hands are doing!

Resources:

Blau, Melinda. *Parenting by Heart: How to Be in Charge, Stay Connected, and Instill Your Values When It Feels Like You've Only Got 15 Minutes a Day.* Reading, MA: Addison Wesley, 1993.

Mackoff, Barbara. *The Art of Self-Renewal.* Los Angeles: Lowell House, 1993.

Olson, B. Kaye. *Energy Secrets for Tired Mothers on the Run.* Deerfield Beach, FL: Health Communications, 1993.

Swiss, Deborah J., and Judith P. Walker. *Women and the Work/Family Dilemma.* New York: Wiley & Sons, Inc., 1993.

Delicious Laughter

Humor is the affectionate communication of insight.
                                        Leo Rosten

Humor sustains us; it helps us to laugh at ourselves and the many predicaments we find ourselves in. Humor communicates common experiences and gives us insight into our lives. It can change our perspective, even our mood. Without it, we would be oh so serious.

For mothers, humor is an essential antidote to stress. Scientists contend that the very act of smiling releases endorphins, "happy hormones," into our system, thus helping to combat the potentially harmful effects of tension on the body. Without a doubt, laughter keeps us sane. But, more than that, it can make us feel alive with delight even on the most difficult days. It can turn a question on its head and tilt our perspective toward the absurd.

Think of all the situations you've found yourself in as a result of motherhood that, had you not added a humorous twist, you might have lost your smile for an indefinite amount of time!

When I was in my second year of nursing my son Alexander, my father's growing discomfort was becoming increasingly evident. "How long are you going to nurse him?" he finally asked one day, unable to hide his concern. "Until he's sixteen," I responded with a straight face. "Sixteen!" he exclaimed. "What are you going to tell his friends?!" Without skipping a beat I told him cheerfully, "That he comes home for lunch!"

My uncle Brian, a father of three, told me a joke when I was in my late twenties that has become funnier with each passing year. It goes something like this: When you first start going out you have sex everywhere. Sex on the kitchen table. Sex on the floor. Everywhere. Then, when you get married, sex is mostly confined to the bedroom. You have bedroom sex. Eventually, after you've had kids, you have hallway sex. You pass each other in the hallway and say, "Screw you!"

As a close friend who is a therapist and mother of one told me recently: "There's one benefit to being a therapist. No matter how difficult my life seems on any given day, I can be assured that someone else will walk into my office and tell me their troubles and I'll think to myself, 'What am I complaining about?!'" The truth is, it could always be worse. And the truth is, laughter always makes it better.

More resources that will keep you laughing:

Ballantyne, Sheila. *Norma Jean the Termite Queen*. New York: Penguin, 1983.

Jackson, Marni. *The Mother Zone*. New York: Henry Holt & Co., 1992.

Kingsolver, Barbara. *The Bean Trees*. New York: Harper & Row, 1988.

Kingsolver, Barbara. *Pigs in Heaven*. New York: HarperCollins, 1993.

Watterson, Bill. *The Calvin and Hobbes Tenth Anniversary Book*. Kansas City, MO: Universal Press Syndicate, 1995.

Watterson, Bill. *The Indispensable Calvin and Hobbes*. Kansas City, MO: Universal Press Syndicate, 1992.

Index

Beth Shannon Wilson (formerly Beth Wilson Saavedra) offers a variety of workshops for women and mothers: Restoring Balance to a Mother's Busy Life (based on her book), Creativity and Self-Expression, Creating Sacred Space, and Exploring Your Treasury of Talents.

Beth is also available to lead Blessing Way ceremonies for expectant mothers based on a rich mixture of spiritual traditions and women's rites of passage.

If you are interested in her workshops and would like to be on her mailing list, please contact her at:

Beth Shannon Wilson
334 State Street, #106-137
Los Altos, CA 94022
(415) 654-1202